Nora Archibald Smith

The Children of the Future

Nora Archibald Smith

The Children of the Future

ISBN/EAN: 9783337215811

Printed in Europe, USA, Canada, Australia, Japan

Cover: Foto ©Lupo / pixelio.de

More available books at **www.hansebooks.com**

CONTENTS[1]

	PAGE
THE STUDY OF CHILDREN	1
TRAINING FOR PARENTHOOD	20
THE CHARM OF THE LILY	31
THE PRIESTLY OFFICE	41
SAND AND THE CHILDREN	57
A DUMB DEVIL	67
AN UNWALLED CITY	76
PERILOUS TIMES	85
A DEVISER OF MISCHIEFS	92
"TELL ME A STORY"	101
THE AUTHENTIC IN KINDERGARTEN TRAINING	114
THE GOSPEL OF WORK	127
THE BROTHERHOOD OF SAINT TUMBLER	143
THE KINDERGARTEN IN NEIGHBORHOOD WORK	158

[1] Many of the above essays first appeared in *The Outlook* and in *Table Talk*, and are here reprinted by the kind permission of the editors. Most of them are considerably extended from their original form, while others have been written for this volume.

THE CHILDREN OF THE FUTURE

THE STUDY OF CHILDREN

"Love the child, and he will reveal himself to you."

WHEN a thoughtful child was asked one day why a certain tree in the garden was so crooked, he responded that he "s'posed somebody must have stepped on it when it was a little fellow." The answer was so philosophic, so unexpectedly rich in its insight into causes, that the questioner may well be pardoned if he was somewhat dismayed, and regarded his companion as another example of the "seers blest,"

> "In whom those truths do rest
> Which we are toiling all our lives to find."

It was but a chance remark, one of those wise things which children often surprise us by saying, but you remember it was the bow drawn at a venture that slew the great King Ahab. Not trees alone are bent and twisted in their growing by carelessness and ignorance, and many a distorted human life attests the truth of the child's saying.

It is only another proof of the infinite scope of the Divine plan that such countless myriads of human beings can be born into the world, all built on the same general lines, and yet differing so widely one from another as to need for their best development climates and training as dissimilar as do the polar bear and the bird of paradise. Through carelessness, through ignorance, through dullness — sometimes, indeed, through sheer wickedness — many children are no better understood by their parents than if they were natives of another planet. Truth to tell, they often appear to many of us to be strangers and foreigners, though how the tiny creatures, born of our own flesh and blood, and nurtured at our hearthstones, can so differ from one another and from their parents is a problem to puzzle the wisest.

Yet, whether this be due to heredity, to prenatal influences, or to the old, old theory of the transmigration of souls, the facts are there, as solid as the hills themselves. Every child differs from every other child as much as one star differeth from another star in glory, and not until this is understood, and training is given to suit the particular case, can we be sure that the budding human life will not be killed, bent, or stunted by misapplied force. Because the father was well brought up by a particular system, there is no reason to suppose that it will succeed with the son; because the eldest daughter has flourished under certain discipline, we need not therefore conclude that it will fit the youngest equally well. The polar bear must be fed on something besides seeds and fruits if he is to be a model of his kind, and the bird of paradise will pine away before he will reconcile himself to a diet of raw flesh.

We cannot devise a plan of education suited to the normal child, and then wind up our own little one and "fix him," as

Richter says, "exactly as if he were an astronomical, hundred-yeared chronometer warranted to show the hours and positions of the planets quite accurately long after our death." We cannot do this, for probably he is not a normal child. He may be an average one, but that is quite a different thing, and it is our first and highest business in life to find out his personal equation as far as we may, — that is, to discover how near he comes to the standard in one direction, how far he overlaps it in another, whether he needs free rein here, curbing there, encouragement in one line, or reproof in a second. True, parents and teachers have always known this to be necessary, but knowing one's duty is not synonymous with performing it, on this planet at any rate.

The mother's intuition in regard to her child is, of course, a great help toward understanding him, though intuition is obviously not enough for this line of work; it needs to be supplemented by thought and study, by careful observation and record.

Child-study as a science is the newest of new things, in this country at least, — only about ten years old as yet in any distinct and systematic form, although Dr. Stanley Hall began his public work in this direction in 1880. When we reflect, however, that 1870 is the Anno Domini of educational development in most countries, and that the first chair of pedagogics in any of our colleges and universities was established little more than a decade ago, we cannot wonder that the allied sciences should have been somewhat slow in gaining public recognition. Before 1880, Perez in France, Preyer in Germany, Darwin in England, with other less known European scientists, had begun to make careful observations of children on various lines, and their books on the subject are of much value. No doubt they helped to awaken public interest in the subject in the United States, though on the whole, as one of the leaders in the movement has said, "child-study is, in a peculiar sense, American."

Perez's "First Three Years of Childhood" and Preyer's "The Infant Mind" are wonderful records of infant development, and by similar labors many mothers might become invaluable helpers in the general work, as well as serve their own interests meantime, by gaining a fuller comprehension of their children.

Friedrich Froebel, the father of child-study, as early as 1841 desired mothers to record in writing the most important facts about each separate child. "It seems to me most necessary," he said, "for the comprehension and for the true treatment of child-nature, that such observations should be made public from time to time, in order that children may become better and better understood in their manifestations, and may therefore be more rightly treated, and that true care and observation of unsophisticated childhood may ever increase."

"Life books" according to Froebel's suggestions have been kept of late years by many mothers, and if all observations are recorded while still fresh, and effort is made that they shall be thoroughly impartial, they can but be of inestimable worth to the child, to the mother, and perhaps, incidentally, to science. In turning the pages of a book of this kind, one is struck, possibly, by the frequent manifestation of such and such a disagreeable trait, not a pleasant thing for a fond parent to note, but much more pleasant to discover now, when there is some hope of correcting it, than to have it to struggle with by and by when it has grown a giant in strength. Again, we may note early tendencies in some specific direction, literary, musical, artistic, mechanical, which are of great service in shaping the child's future career; or, results following well-intentioned discipline which show it to have been entirely mistaken.

Careful records of the physical development of the child, his growth in height and weight, his body girths at different ages, the order in which his muscular movements and their coördinations appear, are frequently of special value to the family physician, and also sometimes serve to indicate coming illness, or some lurking trouble which, though plainly shown by stoppage of growth or loss of weight, may not for a long time declare itself in any other manner. The unfolding of the senses in their order, the progressive manifestations of the emotions, the earliest signs of intellectual life, the development of language, — all these afford rich fields for observation. Mothers who are in doubt as to just what and how to observe will find great help in Mrs. Felix Adler's little hand-book, " Hints for the Scientific Observation and Study of Children," in Mrs. E. R. Jackman's " Outlines for Child-Study," in the Topical Syllabi sent out from Clark University, and those issued by the various associations and magazines devoted to the subject, while they may also get some valuable ideas from Professor A. D. Cromwell's " Practical Child-Study."

It need not be supposed that a creature thus carefully observed is held under a microscope for the process, like some rare insect or botanical specimen. The essence of the observation is that the subject shall be quite unconscious that he is being watched. Of course, as an infant he knows nothing of the record made, and as he grows older it is desirable that he should still be kept ignorant in regard to it. Undoubtedly it is a difficult task to make the observations carefully, veraciously, impartially, and still more difficult to record them before they become dim and uncertain. It would obviously be impossible for an ignorant woman to make observations with scientific method and discrimination; it would be still more out of the question for the unfortunate mother whose nurslings must be left to the care of others while she earns their bread away from home, or for that wretched martyr of the sweating-shops who toils all day and far into the night to keep the breath of life in the beings whom she has brought into the world.

And here is just the opportunity of all

others where women may lend a helping hand to one another. If you are so blessed as to hold the true position of a mother and be the constant companion of your child, you may perhaps, by observing and recording his every manifestation, be of the greatest service in the future to some neglected little one whom you never saw and never will see. Whoever has learned to understand one child thoroughly, whoever has faithfully recorded, as far as she was able to note them, each step in his physical and psychical development, has been a benefactor to all children, if her record is so made as to be intelligible to others. "It is probable," says Sully, "that inquiries into the beginnings of human culture, the origin of language, of primitive ideas and institutions, might derive much more help than they have hitherto from a close scrutiny of the events of childhood."

If this is so, how immeasurably may the education of the future, physical, mental, and moral, gain by the help of intelligent women if they once set themselves thoroughly to understand the children God has given them.

But if this study is to accomplish all that its devotees are prophesying, not mothers only, but physicians and teachers must work together in harmony. The observation of children must not cease at the threshold of kindergarten and school, for here some of the worst offenses against these little ones have been committed.

Take the school-room itself and discover to your dismay how many ailments may be traced directly to overheating, overcrowding, faulty ventilation, bad drainage, and defective lighting. Ask yourself if it is not a disgrace to civilization that maladies should exist, familiarly known and spoken of as "school-bred diseases"? Ought we not to blush when we seat our children, or those of anybody else, on a bench or at a desk where it is impossible to work with the body in a proper position? Ought we to allow for a moment in our schools any system of writing which is likely to produce curvature of the spine, and which does produce it in a large number of cases? Have we not cause to be ashamed if we force children by law to attend the public schools, and then provide them with books so badly printed that they permanently injure the eyes?

These are some of the indictments as to books and school-rooms. Let us see how we may be judged when we consider school curricula and systems of management. Note, of course, that all of these are not by any means bad, many of them in fact being well suited to some children, but the danger in their application lies in that they are not suited to all. The great fault in our school system is that we try to educate pupils in battalions. We do not individualize sufficiently, and the one sweeping reform which we hope that child-study may make, if it does nothing else, is to open people's eyes to the fact that we cannot grow children as we can string-beans, planting them at exactly the same depth, furnishing them with the same fertilizers, and providing them on the same day with twelve dozen dozen bean-poles to run on, all of the same length and diameter, and stuck straight into the ground at rigidly mathematical intervals.

In many of the French and German public schools careful physical measurements are always made and recorded when the child enters, are periodically renewed, and examined regularly by a physician. The sight and hearing are also tested, and advice is given to the parents if anything is found amiss. The child in the French primary school also keeps a copy-book (*cahier mensuel*), in which once every month he writes out his work for the day. He is usually freshly washed and dressed for this grand occasion, and makes his notes in his very best style, knowing that they will be filed away as a record of his progress. Persons interested in the child's mental and physical development can therefore turn to these books at any time and know quite clearly where he stands.

These physical measurements have lately been begun in some schools in this country, and tests of the relative motor-abilities of children, their fatigue-points, etc., have been undertaken, while the testing of the senses is now quite common.

It is objected by those who have no sympathy with child-study that the teacher who pursues such investigations will have little time left for instruction. Push the argument to its extreme and grant the supposition, and it may be replied that a little instruction given under proper conditions to a child whose mental and physical peculiarities are thoroughly known is vastly better than hours spent, for instance, in giving oral science-lessons across a large room to a boy who is two thirds deaf, or a whole year's blackboard work in numbers to one too near-sighted to see a foot beyond his desk. This is what the Spaniards call "preaching in the desert," and to prove that it must be an elocutionary exercise much practiced in this country, well-attested figures can be furnished to show that between one fifth and one fourth of all the pupils in our public schools have defective hearing, and in at least one city of the United States fifty per cent. of the five thousand school-children were found to have defective vision.

Numbers of so-called "dull" and "backward" pupils are such only because of their impaired senses; and when this is recognized, a physician's advice obtained, and conditions changed to meet their needs, they become as bright as others. Many of the school records of such cases are intensely pathetic in the glimpses they give of the long and bitter suffering which these misunderstood human creatures must have endured before the new science came to their aid.

Not defective children alone, however, suffer from bad school methods, for which, by the way, we are more to blame than the teachers. It is well known that a nervously overwrought child, either in school or at home, becomes weak-willed and vacillating, and that mental excitement and strain, such as are caused by high-pressure examinations and rigid marking, are marvelous producers of chorea and hysteria. Continued overexertion in early years means weakened possibilities in adult life. Forcing a child prematurely into the conventional studies of the school may cause arrested development; and, finally, out-of-school study, so universally required, is most injurious in the brain-weariness and loss of sleep it occasions. A fine, strong, well-balanced child can, it is true, go through almost any system of education and come out unscathed, but how about those who are mentally, physically, or morally handicapped for the ordeal? Is it our desire that "even the least of these little ones shall perish"?

If the mother could put into the teacher's hands when she brought her child to school a brief summary of his threefold development for the first six years of life, making particular mention of his habits, disposition, and defects; if the teacher could supplement this by a series of questions, such as are used in some parts of Germany, to determine roughly the contents of the mind before beginning regular instruction — if these two things could always be done, there would be a good working basis on which to found education. Physical measurements made in the school, sense-tests, etc., would follow, and the teacher besides recording them would also keep a record of the pupil along the mental and moral lines. With these in hand, what an insight into individual peculiarities would be gained, how much more wisely and sympathetically children would be dealt with, how much more definite the work would be, and how close and warm would become the relations between teacher and taught! It will be objected that no living man or woman could do this work for a class of sixty members or more save in the sketchiest way. Very true, and when this truth has once sunk deep enough into the minds and hearts of thinking people, the difficulty will doubtless be seen and removed.

It is along all these lines that the help of women is urgently needed. If the women's clubs of this country, now so strong in numbers, so vigorous and influential, would devote themselves for a time absolutely and entirely to the study of children and their needs, to the working children, the pauper children, the feeble-minded and epileptic, the neglected and truant, the delinquent; if they would investigate school hygiene and architecture, school-bred diseases, kindergarten work, its defects and virtues; if they would study normal as well as abnormal children in order to know what training each should rightfully receive, what a wonderful stimulus would be given to education!

In urging upon women subjects connected with child-study for investigation and discussion, it is not to be understood that general culture is therefore undervalued, or a wide knowledge of art, literature, music, philosophy, and science decried. All these things are undoubtedly necessary to full human development; but the children of the world are in the direct and particular charge of the women of the world, and this charge must not be neglected, though all else be laid aside and forgotten.

TRAINING FOR PARENTHOOD

"It's a great pity to see so many people without any children to educate them."

Mr. Herbert Spencer, in his volume on Education, published about thirty years ago, remarked that the training of that day, both in home and school, seemed best fitted to a race of celibates, and predicted that the philosopher of the future, pondering on the educational records of our time, would greatly marvel at the apparent absence of all preparation for the future duties and responsibilities of parenthood.

That this is still measurably true there can be no doubt, though much improvement in this direction has been made in the education of women, at least, in the last twenty years. The whole matter seems so perfectly clear when once it is forcibly presented that one wonders how it could ever have been passed over or neglected. Were the duties of parenthood only "remote contingencies," as Mr. Spencer says, it would, perhaps, be wise not to spend much time in preparation for them; but as they are constantly assumed, why not give them some consideration in the educational plan? The training required would not be absolutely useless should its subject live and die a celibate. Spending years in the patient study of mining when your future career is to be that of an aeronaut might seem, indeed, a fruitless expenditure of labor; but the parental virtues can never be out of place, however life may shape itself, for they are such as belong to the well-rounded, well-developed character.

We cannot entirely rely upon the parental instinct in this matter, be it ever so strong and pure. Although it may be trusted in the normal human being so far as love and protection are concerned, the rearing of children in our complex modern civilization is so delicate and difficult a matter as to necessitate the development of "blind reason" into a higher faculty which shall see clear-eyed the pathway it must tread. If the training is to be given, then the earlier begun the better, since it is not directing the energies into a special channel, but rather a broadening and strengthening of the whole nature.

All roads proverbially lead to Rome, and consideration of this subject brings us inevitably to the kindergarten and what it does in training the future parent. As well try to write a story without a first sentence, as well attempt to frame a melody without an opening bar, as to omit the kindergarten when considering preparation for life in any phase. It is there, and it cannot be ignored; the story cannot be written nor the melody composed till the beginning is made.

You smile at the idea of cultivating the parental virtues in a tiny creature hardly old enough to realize his own personality; and it would indeed be absurd if the tiny creature did not clearly show you, in his unconscious plays, that the deep, indwelling father, mother instinct is already there. The kindergarten, through its marvelous system of songs and games, addresses this instinct from the very beginning. The finger-songs commonly show three generations in sweet relation, — the grandmother and grandfather, the good mother, the kind father, and the little child close beside them; and many of the representations of animal life deal with the nurture and wise care of the young.

If a bird game is being played, one parent broods the younglings in the nest, the other flies over wood and field in search of their food, while both have united in gathering materials for the family home. When the little ones are fully feathered, the parents carefully teach them to fly, and abundant stories and poems further illustrate the lesson taught. The trade games — carpenter, cooper, blacksmith, whatever they may be — not only inculcate the duty of faithful labor, but show that its fruits should not be spent on self alone. "For wife and children dear at home, I'm toiling all day long," says the song, and the child swings his hammer lustily, feeling that he is working for his dear ones as well as for himself.

Since he cannot govern others who has never learned to rule his own spirit, the kindergarten strives to teach self-government, knowing it to be a vital element of character. It aims to teach, by methods quite within the child's grasp, the inexorable relation of cause and effect, and shows him simply that whatsoever a man soweth that shall he also reap. It begins to give him an understanding of the interdependence of all life, and points out to him that his actions are to be considered not only in regard to his own welfare, but as to the way in which they affect others. It further cultivates such virtues as self-respect and perseverance, as well as a willingness to help in bearing the burdens of the weak.

And what does the future parent need more than a strong feeling of the sacredness of family life and the importance of wise care of the young; a knowledge of the value of labor and the proper use of its rewards; a conviction that every deed, good or evil, must have its consequence; and a well-governed spirit realizing relationship to the world?

Alas! many more things are required, but we need not be discouraged, for the kindergarten will aid in bringing them into being.

Does the parent we are training need a stock of that patience which is "a good root," an unfailing store of love, and a fervor of spiritual life which shall warm every shivering soul it touches? Ah, these are the product of years of noble living; but the kindergarten can breathe around the childish life so soft and gentle an atmosphere that the virtues which God has implanted in every human heart must needs wake and stir and struggle upward toward the light.

A wonderful educational idea, the kindergarten, you say. Yes, truly, a revelation of strength and beauty. A blessed place where life can be so nourished! A blessed place indeed — one of the gateways to the millennium! Dwell therein long enough, and you may not dare to doubt it.

You may think what is claimed for Froebel's system here the effervescence of enthusiasm, but I speak that I do know, and from the standpoint of experience. If enthusiasm can live and grow and wax ever stronger through years of practical work and trial, then it would seem, even to the prejudiced observer, that there must be good ground for it to grow in. Undoubtedly there are kindergartens and kindergartens; the spirit is not the same in all of them; but it is no discredit to the heavenly rectitude of the compass if one has never learned to steer one's ship by it.

Yet I am not such a fanatic as to claim that all the noble qualities mentioned can be fully developed in the kindergarten. I only say that the climate thereof is a genial one, where virtues bud as in their native air, and that if the home influences are favorable, and the succeeding gardener a wise one, the little plant can but keep on urging toward the sun.

The school as commonly conducted is not now, and has not been in the past, especially favorable to the development of the virtues needed by the future parent. Law has commonly been imposed from without, rather than developed from within, and the system of credits and marking has fostered a greedy spirit of emulation, rather than respect for work for the work's sake and a willingness to aid the weaker brother. That this has not been true of all schools goes without saying, and meantime a leaven is working which will in time change these matters. May I be pardoned if I suggest that possibly the kindergarten is this leaven, and that its greatest claim to consideration in the future may, perhaps, be found to lie in the influence it has exerted on higher education?

Nowadays, when that higher education is

completed, the young woman frequently pursues some special course or courses, all eminently practical and useful in future motherhood, should she attain unto that dignity. She goes to a cooking-school, she takes up the scientific study of dressmaking, she attends lectures on Housekeeping as a Liberal Art, on Sanitation and Plumbing, on First Aid to the Injured, etc. She studies the treatment of the sick and the care of invalids, or, perhaps best of all, since all these things may be added unto it, she takes a complete course of kindergarten training.

A kindergarten training-school is the only place where a young woman can get a specific preparation for motherhood. During the year or two of study required, the pupil will not only gain a fund of information regarding the wise treatment of infants and young children, but by daily practice, frequently among the poorer classes, will add to her instinctive tenderness and sympathy the wisdom, good judgment, firmness, self-restraint, and devotion to ultimate ideals needed by the true mother. Nor need she fear, be she an absolutely predestinate spinster, that any of this work will be wasted; for, failing offspring of her own, there is no dearth of the world's forsaken children who hunger and thirst for her loving services.

And what is the future father doing meantime? Is he preparing for his possible responsibilities? is he strengthening his shoulders for the burdens which may some time be laid upon them? or is one parent, if that be a good one, supposed to be enough in a family?

With all the educational agencies at our command, could we produce well-rounded characters, self-controlled, self-governing, abounding in love and in aspiration toward the ideal, convinced with heart-conviction of the responsibility of each to all and all to God — could we do all this, nor neglect the cultivation of the imagination and the reason, nor that knowledge which is gained from books, we should produce the ideal parent, who is after all the ideal human being. But none of these things may be done without the coöperation of the ideal home; and the ideal home is not yet, nor will be, until some seventh wave of humanity has rolled the race onward, far beyond its present halting-place.

THE CHARM OF THE LILY

" He who takes the child by the hand takes the mother by the heart."

THERE is a story somewhere of a humble woman who found on her table one day a fair white lily in a sparkling crystal vase. She dwelt with rapture on the purity of the flower and the exquisite lines of the cup that held it, but noting that the light from the dusty window illumined it but faintly, she hastened to wash the glass. The sun then streamed bravely in through the brilliant panes and showed only too plainly the condition of the floor. This remedied, the walls begged for attention, and the charm of the lily worked until the whole house was set in fairest order.

Has not the kindergarten been a lily whose perfume and beauty have been a magic spell working here, working there, changing, beautifying everywhere? At first we thought of Froebel's principles as applied merely to babies of three to six years, and were absorbed in their beauty, their adaptation to childhood, their unerring adjustment of means to ends. Then, as we studied and thought and strove to clear away all obstruction between us and the light, the lily shone revealed in greater fairness, and we knew that its charm had only half been felt by us at first. What it accomplished for babies showed us what might be done for older children, for young girls, and finally for the home and for the parents.

So as an outgrowth of Froebel's principles kitchen-gardens, housekeepers' classes, and sewing-schools were started ; boys' clubs and libraries, evening classes in handiwork of various kinds begun ; training-schools for kindergartners opened, and the work for young people moved on rapidly. But by and by we found that it was not enough to go forward in a straight line, nor even to broaden out like the sides of a triangle as we progressed; a backward reach was also necessary, or, better still, a rotary motion, " unity for the centre, diversity for the circumference," rippling out in ever-widening circles.

We found that, after all, we knew very little about the child if we did not also know his environment, his home, and his family. When we had begun to make acquaintance with these, we saw at once that the highest benefits of the kindergarten could never be felt by the child unless there was a certain amount of coöperation between parents and kindergartner, and unless there was some degree of intelligent comprehension in the home of what the kindergarten was trying to accomplish.

Miss Emily Shirreff, late President of the London Froebel Society, very wisely said in a recent address: " At a later period a school may be better or worse than the home, and the boy or girl may realize the difference and bear it without serious loss; but the little ones are yet too strange to this wonderful world to understand anything.

They feel spiritual influences as they feel the sunshine or the cold; but the natural growth and expansion of their being is arrested if, as they pass from kindergarten to home, they pass from one system of management to another; and change becomes moral waste."

This was instinctively felt by the thoughtful kindergartner, and instinct became insight as meditation and experience brought her closer to the heart of Froebel's principles.

Do not suppose for a moment that utter lack of sympathy between mother and kindergartner and dense ignorance of the aims of the work were, or are, confined to the poorer classes and to the homes whence come the children of the charity kindergartens. Women are women, you know, in every rank of society, and very probably there are as many shallow, weak, careless, stupid, morally obtuse mothers among the rich as among the poor. It is to be supposed that the Lord sends them offspring as an aid in their salvation, and doubtless the idea is a good one, though the practical working of it is rather hard on the children.

The poor mother often sends her child to the kindergarten to get him "off the street," as she says; the well-to-do mother frequently does the same thing to have him out of her way for a time, and cheerfully confesses her motive. Neither parent, perhaps, really believes that the kindergarten has the least moral or intellectual influence upon her child, but she knows him to be safe, sheltered, amused, and happy for a certain number of hours each day, and in moments of discouragement the kindergartner is glad that she acknowledges even this.

One would not wish to be intolerant of the ignorance on educational subjects among the rich and well-to-do, although the faults of people who ought to know better are always additionally exasperating; but the mothers of the educated classes are commonly more anxious to force their children than are the ignorant ones, and more vociferous as to the wickedness of not teaching them to read under six years. Add to this that they quite frequently forbid their little ones to do any clay modeling lest they soil their hands and aprons; protest against their crawling on the floor as caterpillars, or leaping about as frogs, lest they wear out their clothing; and — crowning absurdity! — often decline to send their children to kindergarten at all, "if that Mrs. Thingumbob's children are allowed to come, too."

Dear high-caste mothers (in a land where no caste is supposed to exist), forgive me! I know most of you are saints in the bud, and some of you have even begun to blossom. I know that many of you are thoughtful, earnest, intelligent, and conscientious, but a few drops of acid long ago entered into my blood when the wicked sisters among you began to checkmate the well-intentioned kindergartner, and though the defects I have mentioned are probably only the shadow-side of your virtues, yet the acid is still in my veins, and it will work out now and then. And do not think that I make little of the ignorance, the carelessness, the prejudice, the not infrequent brutality of the mothers of the " other half." I know, I sadly recognize them all; but are not such women something more forgivable, seeing that " they know not what they do " ?

When, then, the wise kindergartner realized the want of connection between her little kingdom and the home, she felt that the parents must somehow be brought into sympathy with her plans, the general result of the existing conditions on the child's progress being much like that of the far-famed frog who climbed eight feet up the well every day and slipped back seven every night.

The thoughtful mother doubtless felt with equal keenness this disheartening condition of things, and the help she brought to the partial solution of the problem must not be ignored.

As soon, however, as kindergartner and mother were thoroughly aroused to the necessity of coöperation, they began to coöperate a little, and the work immediately received an impetus in the right direction. It was never difficult to interest the mother, or even the elusive father, in the surface beauty of the kindergarten, the dainty work, the charming surroundings, the sweet singing, the harmonious movements, the evident happiness. All these any bystander may see, but to persuade him to look below the surface and discover that they are merely outward and visible signs of inward and spiritual graces — ah, that is another matter!

Here and there, then, throughout the country, the kindergartners began to send special invitations to the parents to spend an hour or so with the children and watch them at their work and play. True, the parents had been told before that they would always be welcome at any time, but as "any time" is proverbially "no time," the invitations were seldom accepted.

The mother who had never been quite able heretofore to believe that Mary made her charming inventions entirely by herself, now saw her producing them and absorbed in the joy of creation; the one who had never thought of the kindergarten as anything but play, was amazed at the knowledge of mathematics shown by Johnnie as he folded his papers and built with his blocks; while both gained some valuable new information as to the real inner nature of their little ones, as they watched the progress of the games. The kindergartners gave a word of explanation occasionally as they found time, or moved aside a moment for a bit of quiet talk about the reasons for this and that; but these morsels of information were soon felt to be far from satisfying, and all thoughtful mothers united in a desire for a better understanding of the underlying principles of Froebel's system.

The kindergartners were generally young, frequently inexperienced, and had they trusted to their own knowledge alone, would have felt themselves entirely unfitted to serve as guides in education to those happy women upon whom the privilege of motherhood had been conferred, and who therefore had attained to a kind of spiritual dignity and instinctive wisdom. Yet they were enthusiasts, as all followers of Froebel must be of necessity, and they knew beyond doubt that the study of the kindergarten would train the mother-instinct into insight; would give higher ideals of discipline and of the value of love and reverence in the moral training of the child; would teach the necessity of harmonious purpose throughout the entire scheme of education; would serve as a gateway to wider culture; and finally that the communion of so many earnest women would kindle courage and enthusiasm into a brighter flame in every heart.

And so, indeed, it has proved wherever mothers' meetings, mothers' classes, mothers' conferences, among rich and poor and high and low, have been carried on according to Froebel's principles; and we who believe in the kindergarten are not altogether sure that this, its latest offspring, may not, like the name of Abou ben Adhem, lead all the rest.

THE PRIESTLY OFFICE

"Women should make of their educational calling a priestly office."

It is now about sixty years since Friedrich Froebel, the great benefactor of childhood, began to preach a truth of which he had long been convinced, namely, that "all school education was yet without a proper initial foundation, and that, therefore, until the education of the nursery was reformed, nothing solid and worthy could be attained. The necessity for training intelligent, capable mothers occupied his mind, and the importance of the education of childhood's earliest years became more evident to him than ever before."

It was in 1835 that his idea of a mission to women may be said to have definitely taken shape, and about this time he became so disheartened with the slow progress of his educational ideas in Germany that he seriously thought of emigrating to the United States to establish his system in a new country, presumably less fettered by convention, prejudice, and tradition. He was finally obliged to relinquish this plan, and to struggle on to the end in his own land amid hardships and discouragements such as only a divine enthusiasm could have endured. Froebel could not come to us himself, but no bars of infirmity or chains of circumstance were round his thoughts, and when he sent them forth, they winged their way to the country from which he hoped so much.

It is difficult to say just where and when among us in America the first movement was begun toward that definite work for mothers in connection with the kindergarten, which Froebel preached so long and so earnestly, for when the seeds of certain principles are sown about the same time in many warm and generous hearts, it is probable that there will be an almost simultaneous budding, growth, and flowering.

First in every community came the kindergarten as developed for little children; then the work extended its influence to older boys and girls; next, training-schools for kindergartners were established, and soon these kindergartners felt that their best and most natural helper was the mother, and beckoned her to the magic circle.

. Such was the progress of the movement everywhere, and the pioneers have been so many, that one can hardly see the wood for the trees, though Miss Elizabeth Harrison, of Chicago, must always merit special mention as one of the earliest and most successful in this field. Her personal magnetism and great executive ability not only served her in organizing and setting in motion large mothers' classes under her immediate direction, but she impressed every one of the graduates from her training-school with the vital importance of the mother's coöperation and the necessity of securing it in the beginning as a prime factor in the success of her work. During the winter of 1892-93, four hundred and fifty of the most intelligent women of Chicago were enrolled in Miss Harrison's central and branch classes, and so energetic, wide-awake, rapid, and vigorous is that community that doubtless the number is increased tenfold by this time.

A second renascence has begun in the history of the world — there is a new revival of learning, differing somewhat from the first in that it is felt by women only. There is scarcely a self-respecting woman in our country to-day who does not either attend a class in something — no matter what — or conduct one herself. Eagerly, thirstily, they are everywhere drinking in deep draughts of information on dynamics, therapeutics, hieroglyphics, hydrostatics, mnemonics, Herbartianism, Platonic philosophy, zymotic diseases, and other abstruse subjects with strange and high-sounding names. A fellow kindergartner sat beside a pretty young woman in a car the other day, who looked modest and unassuming and quite like other people, and yet she was reading a pamphlet entitled " The Internal Relations and Taxonomy of the Archæan Terranes of Turkestan, with Notes on the Pre-Paleozoic Surface of the Island of Nova Zembla." My informant copied the title, promptly looking up all the hard words, and could not but throb with pride for her sex as she reflected that one member of it, at least, could read and enjoy this highly condensed extract of literature.

Here and there among these countless clubs and classes for self-improvement, a new subject for study has lately presented itself. It is new, it is useful, it is all-important, and it is deeply interesting to every human being, for it is the scientific study of childhood. " A child, an immortal being," as one of our wise kindergartners says, " is certainly as legitimate an object of respectful study as a starfish, or a microbe, or a plant. He is as important as a freshly exhumed hieroglyphic stone, or a bone of an extinct species, and is not he, ' the living poem,' worthy of as careful and concentrated thought as the masterpieces of literature or the languages of foreign countries?"

One cannot deny that these things are useful and legitimate objects of study, but the child in his heredity, his processes of development, his possibilities for good or evil, his relations to society, is supremely more important; and wherever that fact is recognized and wherever women have banded themselves together for the study of child-culture, it will be found, I think, that the kindergarten influence is behind the movement.

This study of the "science of motherhood," as Froebel calls it, may be greatly varied in scope and method, according as it is taken up by women of thought and cultivation, or by the poor hard-working mothers, many of them very ignorant, many of them speaking but little English, who form the classes in the free kindergartens. To all women, however, rich or poor, wise or ignorant, married or unmarried, the study can but bring added culture, added self-knowledge, greater reverence, thoughtfulness, and tenderness, deeper feeling of responsibility, and wider sense of human relationships.

Each kindergartner or leader in the child-study clubs would naturally conduct her classes according to her own mental bias and the trend of her strongest moral convictions, but any course for cultivated women embraces all, or the greater part, of the following subjects: —

1. The theory of child-culture as found in Froebel's "Mutter und Kose-Lieder," a book little known outside of kindergarten circles, but occupying a unique place in literature, representing as it does the typical experiences of childhood.

2. A critical study of Froebel's connected series of play-material, or his "Gifts and Occupations," with some practical work upon each one of them.

3. Lectures on the representative plays of childhood, on the kindergarten games and songs, their meaning and value, and in this connection the learning and singing of suitable songs for the home and nursery.

4. Lectures on story-telling as an art, and as a science, with suggestions on children's literature and the learning of typical stories.

Talks on moral and physical training, on discipline, on intermediate and higher education, and on the scientific study and observation of children form part of the course also, being as varied and extensive as the time of the class and the wisdom of the leader admit.

Informal meetings are also arranged, to which mothers may bring vexed questions, where matters may be talked over in friendly council, where the experience of the many may be placed at the service of the one, where suggestions may be made as to helpful reading-matter in the line of the work and advice given as to useful home and nursery occupations.

The long-continued and beautiful work in the mothers' classes of the Chicago Kindergarten College culminated not long ago in an enthusiastic public conference, for which special railroad rates were arranged, and whose closing meeting was attended by eight hundred parents. That convocation might perhaps justly be called an epoch in the history of education, for though other specialists have come together for, lo, these many years, to speak and to hear wisdom upon the culture of vines, and trees, and flowers, and horses, and dogs, and cattle, and poultry, yet never before had mothers met in any numbers for the scientific study of the early years of childhood. Three daily sessions were held during this conference, and at the close of the first day it was found necessary to provide an additional room for overflow meetings, and a larger hall for the evening assemblies. Artists, psychologists, physicians, and kindergarten training-teachers addressed the mothers, who were keenly appreciative of the value of the occasion, and free and unconstrained in query and discussion. Some of the subjects taken up were, Pre-Natal Influences, Influence of Nursery Appointments, Clothing and Food of Young Children, Stories and their Psychological Meaning, Constructive and Destructive Games, Home Training and Discipline, Applied Psychology and Kindergarten Principles.

The interest felt in this first conference has inspired many other companies of women to engage in similar work, and its success doubtless led in a measure to the convening of the First National Congress of Mothers, held in the capital of our country last winter.[1]

There were delegates at this Washington meeting from all parts of the United States and from Canada, while many of the leading American educators, both men and women, were in daily attendance.

The subjects discussed were eminently practical: The Care, the Food, the Mental and Moral Education of Children; Preparation for Motherhood; The Duties of Motherhood; and what might be called the Public Responsibilities of Mothers. The audience was chiefly made up of re-

[1] February 17–19, 1897.

presentatives from normal and free kindergarten associations, Women's Christian Temperance Unions, benevolent organizations, educational and industrial organizations, and the Federation of Women's Clubs; while the church was represented largely by mission workers and the King's Daughters. The addresses for the most part were educational, one resolution only being offered, and passed unanimously by a rising vote. This was in favor of admitting into the homes of our country "only those periodicals which inspire to noble thought and deed."

Now, while some may question the advisability of a National Congress of Mothers, no one, probably, will doubt the desirability of local mothers' meetings, designed for the exchange of experiences, for the study of the problems of childhood and of education, and of the community problems that affect home life.

This training the kindergarten has begun to give to mothers, thus preparing them for what Froebel calls "their priestly office," the courses sketched above being intended for women of comparative leisure and education, and needing modification in management and in details for the hard-worked, unlettered women who attend the free kindergarten classes. These humble household priestesses can give no time to outside study, even if they knew how to pursue it, and the talks and lectures for their benefit must be briefer, simpler, and cover a more restricted field of subjects. The meetings, too, in distinction from the study-clubs already described, have a social air about them which is carefully fostered by the kindergartner in order to give a little innocent gayety to these dull, imprisoned lives. The mothers are formally invited, in notes sent by the children, to be present on a certain afternoon, and the kindergartner who is to be the speaker puts on her prettiest gown for the occasion. In certain kindergartens in the West, the assembly room is made into a bower of flowers and vines, and bouquets are frequently provided for the guests to take home; but that is in bounteous California, where blossoms may be had for the asking. In the same kindergartens, too, as a large Housekeeper's Class is one of the branches of the work, they have a little maid of ten or twelve years, neatly attired in cap and apron, to open the door for the visitors and show them to their seats.

At all these meetings, no matter where they are held, some light refreshment is served; and when the mothers enter, they see a flower-trimmed table spread with a shining white cloth, and set with pretty cups and saucers, bright spoons, and a dainty spirit lamp and kettle. Then when the talk is over, the kindergartner and her assistants serve tea, coffee, or chocolate with seed-cakes, wafers, or cookies, and thus the occasion becomes a social event, a real afternoon tea, but much more delightful and inspiring than such functions are commonly found to be.

The women are somewhat shy and embarrassed at first, but this is soon overcome as they grow better acquainted with the kindergartner and with one another, and gradually learn the purpose of the meetings. It will be a cosmopolitan audience thus gathered together in any of our free kindergartens, and somewhat uncongenial in its elements, comprising, as it does, Italians, Germans, French, Irish, Scandinavians, Hebrews, Africans, a few native-born Americans possibly, and perhaps even some wanderers from Syria or Armenia. None are too foreign, however, to be pleased and attentive; some evidently both understand and enjoy the simple address, some light up at intervals, others get one or two ideas only; but, after all, this might be said of any audience, for when the flow of our thoughts to our fellow creatures is not blocked by ignorance or dullness, it is as apt to be impeded by prejudice, thoughtlessness, and abstraction in other matters.

All the mothers have seen the kindergarten work and play, but they now for the first time are led to understand their meaning. At one meeting, perhaps, they are shown the first few gifts, — the kindergartner explaining simply their mathematical, architectural, and artistic value, and then giving them to the members of the class, who follow dictations as well as may be, and thus get some idea of both theory and practice. Another meeting is devoted to the simpler hand-work with explanations and illustrations; another to story-telling and its value, when one or two useful stories manifolded on the hectograph or mimeograph are presented to the mothers. On another occasion, possibly, Froebel's games and songs are discussed, the kindergartner, with her assistants, drawing the guests to the circle and persuading them to play some of the more familiar ones.

Talks are also given on such subjects as The New Baby, Children's Diseases and Remedies, Children's Food and Clothing, The Mother as an Example, Punishments and Rewards, The True Discipline, Moral and Religious Training, Courtesy, Truth-Tell ing, etc. ; the remarks being brief and clear and designed to lead to subsequent expression of opinion from the audience.

Think of the incomparable value of such meetings to these shut-in women, whose eyes have never learned to look beyond the narrow streets in which they live, who never read, who never see fine pictures or hear sweet music, who have absolutely nothing around them which will quicken in their souls the flame of aspiration. Should a dozen, a score, a hundred, mothers' meetings only lighten for a time the burden laid on one of those tired backs; only lift for a little the drooping corners of those sad, hard mouths; only give those dull, short-sighted eyes one swift glimpse into the dazzling face of the ideal, they would even then have served their purpose, they would have done a bit of the world's work and a bit worth doing.

SAND AND THE CHILDREN

"The plays of childhood have the mightiest influence on the maintenance or non-maintenance of laws."

IN a daily paper, not long ago, appeared the following brief article : —

SAND-HILLS WANTED FOR CHILDREN.

The Brotherhood of the Kingdom has applied to the Park Board to provide sand-hills in various places in the city for the use of little children. Those who are urging this innovation in New York life say : —

"In Berlin and other Continental cities, sand-hills are a long-established feature of the parks. In the 'Thiergarten' there are large spaces reserved for that purpose; the children dig to their hearts' content while the nurses and mothers sit reading and talking, with an occasional glance at their charges. In the smaller parks in the centre of the city there are sand-hills on every corner, and they are often so crowded with children that they look more like little heaps of humanity than heaps of sand.

"Sand-hills could be provided at the ends of the several greens in Central Park, at the Mall, and in the smaller parks of the city, like Bryant Park and Tompkins Square. The expense of providing and occasionally renewing them would be slight, and they would require little care, except occasionally sweeping back the sand. Altogether it would be hard to find an improvement giving so much pleasure for so little outlay, and to the *worthiest and most important class of our citizens.*"

I have taken the liberty of italicizing eight words in the above quotation, because of the delicious novelty of the phrase. I have never doubted myself that the children were the most important class of our citizens — still less that they were the most worthy; but I have not been accustomed heretofore to find my attitude of mind adopted unconditionally by the grown-up world. Dear American citizens of the future, the millennium is already dawning, if we have begun to realize just how worthy and how important you really are!

Germany seems in many respects to offer a simpler, freer, more truly childlike life to its little ones than is found in our country. The German people have grown to understand them more thoroughly than we have ever taken time to do, and, understanding, are better able to provide for their natural, instinctive wants. A land that has produced such writers of children's stories as the Grimm brothers, such a composer of children's songs as Reinecke, such a painter of child-pictures as Meyer von Bremen, such a child-lover and child-interpreter as Froebel, may be trusted to know what means of play and occupation are best suited to the simple, normal child. We are not surprised, therefore, when we read of the sand-hills in the "Thiergarten" and the smaller parks of Berlin, for these only minister to the strong desire, the natural instinct, to dig and to grub in the earth, shown by every young human animal, and noted by every discriminating observer.

That this is a universal instinct no effort need be made to prove, for a momentary recollection of one's own childhood and a glance out upon the world will furnish all needed evidence of the statement.

Who is so old that he cannot recall the soft, cool touch of the sand as he patted and smoothed it, the fascinating way in which it slipped through the fingers when poured from one hand into another, the endless joy of digging into its yellow depths, the facility with which it could be heaped into mountain chains, hollowed into valleys, moulded into forts, and thrown up into breastworks?

Who has forgotten the delicate cakes and pies he used to make of sand, or, when it was well smoothed, how he delighted to impress his hand upon the yielding surface, or use it for a drawing-board, and sketch figures and letters and pictures upon it?

There is no play-material which is at once so responsive, so indestructible, so cheap, and so universally enjoyed, and there is nothing which city children, at least, have so little opportunity to use.

The delicately nurtured child is often warned away from sand-heaps for fear of soiled hands and clothing, for, as somebody says, "Thou shalt not make thyself dirty" is the first maternal commandment.

The children of the poor, on the contrary, have no access to any such clean and attractive play-material, save as they see it in small quantities on the sand-tables of the free kindergartens. Those institutions in most of our large cities, however, bear, unfortunately, so slight a proportion to the number of children of kindergarten age that they can hardly be considered in the problem. In many of the German kindergartens, that of the Pestalozzi-Froebel House for instance, a large sand-garden shaded by trees is provided, large enough for a number of children to play in at once, and with sufficient quantity of sand to allow unlimited digging, grubbing, mining, gardening, and filling of small pails and carts.

Most American kindergartens consider themselves blessed if they are possessed of a sand-table, which is merely a deep, water-tight box on stout legs, large enough for a dozen small persons to gather about, and filled with sand to within a few inches of the top. Around this box the children cluster and engage in all kinds of delightful plays under the friendly guidance of the kindergartner. At first they dig into the sand, cover and uncover their hands with it, pour it through their fingers, heap it up and level it again; then they smooth it and press wooden balls deep down in it, perhaps, making quantities of soft, rounded birds' nests. On some other occasion paths and roads are laid out and "make-believe" gardens planted; and by and by, when the workers have grown more expert, the whole surface is laid out to represent a village, with its surroundings of mountains, hills, lakes, and rivers. The children do all the work in company, dividing the labor according to their different abilities, and afterwards, with their blocks and sticks, erect the houses, the public buildings, fence the gardens and barnyards, and add life to the scene by planting miniature trees along the roadsides and stationing toy sheep and cows in the fields. By such means they taste the never-failing joy of playing in the sand, learn practically to know the value of coöperation, and gain an idea of natural formations which is most valuable in the school when the study of geography is begun. There, too, the sand-table is sometimes used, its value in geography-teaching being recognized in some quarters. But even though every child went to a kindergarten and subsequently to school (which supposition, alas! is worlds away from truth), and even if sand were used in both places, the desirability of large sand-heaps in squares or courts or parks, for free, unguided play, would not therefore be lessened. The universal, healthy delight in real contact with the earth, the joy of digging and heaping, the keen interest in moulding a responsive substance, in working out ideas with an easily handled material — all these impulses need gratification on a larger scale than is practical in kindergarten and school, and need, too, a field where they can unfold spontaneously and with absolute freedom.

Those who have read Dr. Stanley Hall's suggestive article, "The Story of a Sand-Pile,"[1] will already have an idea of the wealth of valuable knowledge in various directions which may be gained by free play in the sand. There are now, we are told, throngs of children of school age in our growing American cities who do not attend school, and this largely because there is no room for them. What are these children doing, where are they playing, and what are they playing with? It is obvious that they

[1] E. L. Kellogg & Co.

cannot be the children of the rich, or of the well-to-do portion of the population; and it is equally obvious that a large proportion of them are either too young or too incapable to be at work, or that there is not as yet any necessity for their employment. Nobody who knows children supposes that they are sitting at home with folded hands; particularly when home means two or three small rooms already overcrowded with furniture and babies and washtubs, and very deficient in light and air. But what *are* they doing — this immense army of school age, and the uncounted thousands a little younger, scarcely out of babyhood, and yet old enough to be in the streets? Have they any playgrounds, have even the school-children themselves any proper place to play, in or out of school hours; in fine, have the children of the poor any one thing to do out of doors which is simple and normal and healthful? Take a walk through the crowded streets where babies most do congregate, and settle the question for yourself. You are fortunate if you are able to bring back even the hint of an affirmative answer.

There are some improved tenements, lately erected in Brooklyn, which are built around a square, half of which is kept green as a park, and the other half provided with heaps of sand for children. The janitor merely shovels the sand into fresh heaps when the blithe workers have gone, but takes no other charge of the play, and the policemen stationed in the neighborhood report that *no windows have been broken there* since the sand-piles were established.

Would not a sand-pile placed in some appropriate spot and devoted to the use of children be as fitting a memorial to the beloved as a stained-glass window? It would come considerably cheaper as an investment in the beginning, and the interest on it would be — how much greater in the end?

A DUMB DEVIL

"This kind goeth not out but by prayer and fasting."

THE fire won't burn! It smoulders and hisses and sighs gloomily about the logs. Now and then it sends up a blunt arrow of flame which has no successor; now and then it blows a great puff of smoke in your face as you kneel beside it shivering. You feed it with kindling which it seizes upon, chars, and throws aside. It resists poking, resists blowing, resists rearrangement. It won't do anything, — not even go out, but glowers at you with one defiant eye as you sink exhausted on the hearth.

The world is cold and damp outside and warmth and comfort are sorely needed, but there you crouch with hands begrimed, in front of the blackened wood and the gray ashes.

You are chilled and tired and unhappy. The fire won't burn!

There is nothing more depressing in a household than that peculiarly unpleasant form of temper which we call sulkiness. It lowers the barometer of happiness as effectually as a northeast storm, and its noxious vapors spread abroad as quickly as the fumes of burning sulphur.

It is another proof of the exquisite sensitiveness of the moral atmosphere that wraps us round that it can be so easily affected by the silent mood of another person, though that person be but a rebellious child afar in the nursery, or a mutinous cook glooming in the kitchen.

Words, after all, play a small part in intercommunication, being as often used to conceal thought as to express it; but no one, not even the household dog, can fail to interpret rightly the heavy silence, the lowering brow, the changed color, and the brooding eye of a human creature in the sulks.

I confess that the temperament which is wont to hang out these and similar storm-signals is to my mind a supremely difficult one to deal with, and one which I should approach with a well-defined sinking at the heart. I do not say that it is hopeless of improvement, but the saving work must be begun very early and must rest upon a well-defined diagnosis of the disease, one of its overwhelming difficulties being that the patient resists remedies much as if he were afflicted with tetanus, while inquiry into his symptoms and the causes of his suffering is as profitable as to question the Sphinx.

When does this temperament begin to show itself? Certainly not as early as determined self-will or capability of fierce passion. It cannot appear before the birth of self-consciousness, for it commonly has its root in the supposed perception of injury to self; nor can it come before the age when some reasoning power and conscious command of memory have been attained, for its daily food is real or fancied grievances which the mind perceives, records, and will not or cannot forget.

One of the causes of sulkiness is frequently to be found in a violated sense of justice. The child perceives, often with too much reason, that he is treated unfairly, that his misdeeds are punished capriciously, or more heavily than they deserve, or perhaps that he is corrected for a fault which another member of the family may commit with impunity. He knows that he is weak and cannot avenge himself, he is unable by the very constitution of his being to cry aloud for redress, and the sense of wrong filters slowly into his heart, corroding everything it touches.

It is easily possible, of course, that this may be the state of the case; but, on the other hand, it is quite as likely that his wrongs are largely imaginary, — ordinary occurrences seen with a jaundiced eye. The lunatic who fancies himself a king is exposed to a thousand assaults of rank and cruel wounds of dignity from his supposititious subjects, and the child who regards himself as the centre of the universe is easily wounded in self-love, and bears constantly about with him that inconvenient bit of luggage known as " a chip on the shoulder."

There is no denying, I think, that egotism has much to do with sulkiness, and that if the child (or the grown person) could be led to have a juster idea of himself, if he could be persuaded to think less of his own wrongs and give some attention to other people's rights, his malady would be in a fair way of being cured.

Let us be charitable, however, and remember that what may appear like sulkiness is sometimes a dark and gloomy habit of mind which is consequent on physical weakness, or upon great ante-natal depression on the mother's part. I was discussing the subject the other day with an observant old lady from New England, who shrewdly remarked, " Oh, half the time the children ain't a mite to blame for their sulky tempers. Some of 'em are down-hearted from the start. Why, I knew of a baby down to Hardscrabble that was discouraged when it wa'n't but two days old."

The sullen child, if he is to be cured, needs more than any other to be surrounded with silent love, — waves of it, billows of it, floods of it, warm and grateful as a tropic ocean. Gloom, discouragement, rebellion, bitterness, cannot long endure in that sweet encompassment, and the child must be led to feel to the very depths of his selfish, tortured heart that in one quarter, at least, there will be inexhaustible mercy and tenderness and sympathy. And this does not mean that he is to be humored, or petted, or his misdeeds overlooked, — it only means that such a child needs absolute certainty of love somewhere, lest he become another Cain, jealous and murderous as the first one. He must be treated with strict and absolute justice, which is entirely compatible with the highest kind of love; and he must be made happy with suitable companionship and occupation. "Cross Patch," of childish rhyme, who sat by the fire to spin, doubtless had sufficient occupation, but we note that she drew the latch before she began to turn her wheel. This is of all things what the sulky child must not be suffered to do; he must never draw the latch and seclude himself to brood over his wrongs.

Now, all these things — need of love, appropriate discipline, happiness, suitable companionship, and occupation — are so many demands of the child's nature which have but one source of supply at this stage of his development, and that is the kindergarten. It is not obtruded here, you observe, — it obtrudes itself, like a massive boulder sleeping under deep brown masses of pine needles, — softly covered and yet heaving a strong shoulder through the fragrant coverlid. A well-ordered kindergarten seems indeed to be by far the most effective agency for dealing with the beginnings of these moral evils, and one might as well attempt to ignore it as to ignore the water that bears up the yacht, or the flagstaff that holds the banner.

There are no children on earth to whom the kindergarten is such a blessing as the selfish and the sulky ones, and to these it comes like an angel of deliverance. It is because the devil which dominates the sulky child is a dumb one, and therefore deaf, that he is so difficult to cast out. He cannot hear reason and he has never learned to speak it, and every avenue of self-expression which we open is for this cause a distinct and separate gain. The child draws and colors, moulds, builds, and invents, and the demon in his heart begins to oppress him less. He uses his voice and moves his body in song and game, and still greater relief is felt; he is led to express a thought or an opinion through his absorption in his work; and before long he is free, happy, and unconscious. He is in the society of his equals, those who are of like age and strength and interests; he has occupation which his soul loves; and he is, for the most part, too busy to brood, and too interested in other things and people to think about himself. If the kindergarten is what it should be, he is always treated fairly; and should he give way to his besetting sin at any time, the disapproval of the small world about him, representing public opinion, is more keenly felt than the disapproval of his mother. If his body is kept in good condition by proper food and sleep, if he has plenty of outdoor exercise, which is especially essential to his temperament, if he is loved well and wisely at home, and if he is made happy, busy, and self-forgetful in a good kindergarten, then we may have every hope that his difficulties of temper will gradually be overcome. But if these things be neglected, or begun too late, then all the fasting and prayer of the Trappist monks will scarce avail to exorcise the dumb devil of sulkiness.

AN UNWALLED CITY

"He that hath no rule over his own spirit is like a city that is broken down and without walls."

As there are many kinds of fire, from the quick crackle of dry sticks to the mighty sweep and roar of the full-fed blaze, or the sulky sputter and hiss that show wet wood, so there are many varieties of the passionate temper in children, each one needing separate analysis and separate mode of treatment.

To begin at the beginning, all observant mothers will agree that the first manifestations of this temper occur at a very early age, some time before short clothes have been considered, and that remedies for it are often applied entirely too late. I can certainly testify from wide experience that a child of three years may already have developed a capacity for wild, unreasoning rage that would shame a mad bull or a Hyrcan tiger. Had not the parents been adherents of the too common opinion that a baby's faults are very trifling things, which may be left to correction in after years, this capacity might already have been somewhat lessened.

A child at the height of one of these accesses of rage is, in truth, an appalling object. Prone on the floor, kicking and stamping, flushed and screaming, biting and striking whatever hand is held out to him, swearing, if he be a child of the street, until the air is thick with sulphurous fumes, or, even worse, holding his breath until his face grows black and the eyes start from his head — he seems, in truth, a child no longer, but a creature under demoniacal possession. That the demon is one of his own rearing, tenderly nursed until it has attained its present monstrous strength, is of no moment, for what foes can a man have which shall be worse than those of his own household?

What may be done for him at the moment? Shall we punish him? As well put out a fire with kerosene. Shall we reason with him? As well reason with Vesuvius in full flow. Shall we try to soothe him with kind words and caresses? As well pat a cyclone on the back and coax it to be still. No; I assert boldly that the only thing to be done at this juncture is to let him alone, to leave the room, if there be another room, and in some remote corner of the house offer up a small prayer for the souls of his ancestors (including ourselves), who undoubtedly have some responsibility for the phenomena we have just witnessed.

In spite, however, of the fact that these blind furies are evil to look upon, as much so as convulsions, which they somewhat resemble, the child who is torn by them need not be at all despaired of. There are many faults which are far more difficult to cure, and this one commonly springs from no radical defect of nature, but rather from a big, savage force somewhere which needs regulating and putting to use. The passionate temper in children is regarded more seriously, perhaps, because it is so ill to live with. Isaiah says in regard to the pride of Sennacherib, "Because thy rage against me and thy tumult is come up into mine ears, *therefore* I will put my hook in thy nose and my bridle in thy lips," the inference being that if the noise of that rage had not been so unpleasant he would have made less effort at bridling and taming. So it is sometimes with the unfortunate child of passionate temper, who, because his tumult so dins at the ears, gets a thousand times more reproof and punishment than his quiet little brother, whose faults lie deep and black at the bottom of the still pool of his nature.

Let us consider for a moment the causes of this fiery passion; for, knowing these, it is easier to give relief. There is no doubt that violent fits of rage in children sometimes spring from purely physical causes. An eminent physician says that a child is often whipped for so-called "naughtiness," when what he needs is bed and a dose of medicine; and grown people, who know how difficult it frequently is to control the temper in sickness, can well believe this to be true. But, excluding temporary ailments, the child may be in a low-toned, neurasthenic condition, when his passions are all on the surface, when everything and everybody is vexatious, and when he has absolutely no strength of will with which to resist the suggestions of his temper. In such a case nothing but careful and hygienic treatment can bring the body to its normal state and restore the balance of the emotions.

There are other cases in which unreasonable rage springs from some slight brain trouble, a pressure on some delicate fibre here, a nerve out of order there, some portion of the exquisite mechanism a little wrong somewhere. Persons familiar with the mysterious disease of epilepsy know that uncontrollable attacks of rage are among its common symptoms, and if there seems no other cause for violent temper in a child, this one should at least be considered.

Setting aside disorders of brain and nerve and body, and considering the normally healthy human creature, we cannot but see that home training is sometimes directly responsible for these manifestations of temper. Perhaps the child has been accustomed to note, ever since he could note anything, that violent screaming always brought what he wanted; perhaps the very first time he gave way to rage he observed that parents and guardians flew like leaves before the blast, and the way was cleared for his desires; perhaps he has never been taught self-control in any appetite; perhaps he has been spoiled and petted and humored until he is a monster of caprice. If any of these suppositions be true, alas for the sufferer! for his only help will be within his own bosom, and in the long stretch of years before he learns the necessity of self-control the temper-demon will gain appalling strength.

There are possibilities, too, that the child has a strong will which some injudicious person has been trying to break, that he has been continually over-punished, that his keen sense of justice has been wounded until it cries out in pain, or that he has been fed on those "grievous words" which never fail to "stir up anger."

But here he is as we have made him, and what shall we do for him now? Obviously, find out the cause of the disease, if possible, and, if we be the offenders, repent it in anguish and bitterness, and strive to cast out the devils which we ourselves invited in.

In the first place — and this is not weakness, but common sense — try not to enter into controversies with him, avoid provocation, and endeavor to ward off absolute issues. Distract his attention, try to get the desired result in some other way, but give no room for an outburst of temper if it can be avoided, remembering that every stone broken from the city's walls renders it more defenseless.

Do not fret him with groundless prohibitions, do not speak to him quickly and sharply, and never meet passion with passion. If you punish him when you are angry, he clearly sees that he, because he is small and weak, is being chastised for the same fault which you, being large and strong, may commit with impunity.

After one of these outbursts of temper, do not reprove and admonish the rebel until he is rested. The storm descended like a very hurricane upon the waters of his spirit, and the noise of the waves must be stilled before the mind can listen to reason. When the sun comes out, after the storm, is the time to note wreckage and take measures for future safety. Select some quiet, happy hour, then, in which you can gently warn him of his besetting sin, and teach him to be on his guard against it. Until this time comes, and he is in a condition for counsel and punishment, an atmosphere of grief and disapproval may be made to encompass him, which he will feel more keenly than spoken words. And when the time for punishment does come, let us try to make it, as far as possible, the natural penalty, that which is the inevitable effect of given cause; for, as "face answereth to face in water," so the feeling of justice within the child to the eternal justice of world-law.

Finally, let us be patient, but firm and unceasingly watchful, and let slip no opportunity for teaching self-control and cultivating strength of will; for we must remember that a passionate temper, if not early brought under restraint, is as dangerous a thing as a powder-magazine, differing only in that it needs no outside aid to produce an explosion, but can manufacture and apply its own igniting power.

PERILOUS TIMES

"In the last days perilous times shall come, for men shall be lovers of their own selves."

ON looking over the Concordance one day, for a fit text from which to preach a sermon on selfishness, I was struck by the fact that the writers of the New Testament had exactly six times as much to say upon the subject as had the early priests and kings and prophets. Is selfishness a product of civilization then? Hardly that, for its foundation-stones, self-preservation, interest in self, love of self, are primitive instincts and absolutely necessary ones.

The passion must always have existed and doubtless was a thousandfold stronger in the childhood of the world, but it was probably so much the normal state that no one thought of taking measures against it; as, were it customary for all to suffer from smallpox, no one would think of vaccination.

When man had outgrown the animal state in which self-preservation was his first law, stray beams of thought for others began now and then to shine in upon the darkness of his soul, but it was left for the great Teacher of all time to bring the full glory of the sunlight when He commanded us to love our neighbors as ourselves and when He uttered the immortal paradox, "He that loseth his life for my sake shall find it."

The very young child, like his kinsfolk the animals and his far-away brother in the Dark Ages, commonly looks at life from the standpoint of his own desires and necessities, and has as yet little interest in or sympathy with the feelings of any one else. This is normal and necessary if life is to be well nourished; and it is unwise to force upon him too early the duty of altruism, which belongs to a later ethical period. The fact that the word *altruism* is comparatively a new one, grown into popular use within the memory of some of us, shows that the feeling it describes has not long been widespread, and is another evidence that we must not expect too much from the child in this direction.

We need not be over-anxious, then, if baby finds himself an all-engrossing subject in his earliest years; but, lest this self-interest become a passion, we must watch him carefully as he grows older, and surround him with an atmosphere which will gently, unobtrusively, suggest to him the interests of others.

Of all the evil passions which lurk within the breast of man, surely there is none so black and hateful as selfishness; and not only is it to be feared in itself, but because it is the mother of the whole Satanic brood of vices. A modern writer says: "Selfishness is the fault most impossible to forgive or excuse, since it springs neither from an error of judgment nor from the exaggeration of a generous motive. . . . It is the result of a cold-blooded, self-concentrated system of calculation, which narrows the sympathies and degenerates the mental powers."

Great capabilities for it lie in every nature — no, I may not make so broad a statement, for now and then one meets

> "a purity of soul
> That will not take pollution, ermine-like
> Armed from dishonor by its own soft snow."

Yet these are the exceptions, and the ordinary, strong, healthy, hearty child starts in life with almost as full an equipment of possibilities for evil as for good.

The root of selfishness is doubtless there; but the influences which surround the tiny human being will determine whether it shall lie sleeping underground or send up shoots of rank luxuriance. Too complete devotion in the parents, too absolute forgetfulness of self on their part, wakens no similar passion in the child, but rather the opposite feeling. To deny ourselves the pleasure of self-denial towards him is often the wisest course; and to attempt to bear all his troubles, to save him every effort, to bend our wills to his, to make all sacrifices for him, expecting none in return — this is to make of him a very Juggernaut, whose triumphal car will one day ride over our prostrate bodies. Felix Adler says, in his remarkable pamphlet on "Parents and Children:" "The care of children is the great means of stimulating and preserving unselfishness in the world. The love of children is the great balance-wheel that counteracts the strong tendency towards egotism." The thought is as true as it is beautiful, but some of us need to be careful lest we cultivate our own plant of self-sacrifice at the expense of the child's. Unselfishness is a habit of mind which may be developed, and there are a thousand simple ways in which the training may be begun even in the earliest days of existence. A bit of some dainty given up for love's sake, a miniature task performed for some one, an errand within the house which baby feet may easily perform, a temporary sharing of playthings with a tiny visitor, the tending of plants, the caring for pet animals — all these are ordinary daily happenings which may easily be put within the reach of any child, and which are the beginning of life's service to life.

It is absolutely essential, as Froebel says, to give outward form to the loving thoughts that stir within the child's heart, remembering that love which gains no expression either in thought or action is love which droops and dies away. Here, steadily, surely, strongly as the river sweeps to the ocean, the subject brings me to the kindergarten.

There is no spot on this earth, nor in any other star that God has made, so absolutely and eternally fitted to teach unselfishness as is that " free republic of childhood " where the principles of Froebel hold their sway, for no other educator has ever so felt the " inseparable dependency of all spirits upon one another's being and their essential and perfect depending on their Creator's."

He knew, as Carlyle says, that "each individual person is a part of the great venous-arterial stream that circulates through all Space and all Time," and the whole fabric of the kindergarten is held together by his recognition of that truth. The very circle in which the children sing and play, the games in which no one may usurp another's place, the thought that underlies them, which is the inseparable connection of all life, the work in common, the labor gladly done for others, the care for the weaker children, the aid given to those younger and less advanced, the nurture of plants and animals — all these are so many air-currents, which taken together make a mighty wind blowing away the vice of selfishness like a noxious vapor. Send the selfish child to the true kindergarten, keep him in the life-giving atmosphere at any cost, and if the springs of altruism in your own heart be exhausted, visit it yourself, that you may see in miniature "a perfect union in which no man can labor for himself without laboring at the same time for all others."

A DEVISER OF MISCHIEFS

"Thy tongue deviseth mischiefs; like a sharp razor, working deceitfully."

THE word *lie* is a very ugly one, — doubtless not uglier than the thing itself, but too harsh to describe some of the untruths of children, which can scarcely be judged by the same standard as those of grown people. The lies (so called) of these little ones need long and careful observation, and form a most important object of study, because of the possibility of discovering the causes which produce them, applying remedies and using the experience gained, in the treatment of other delinquents.

Speaking from long and close observation, from introspection, and from conversation with parents, I should say that untruthfulness in early years is commonly due to one of the following causes : —

A DEVISER OF MISCHIEFS 93

Imitation. Remember that imitation is one of the four fundamental instincts of childhood, and if the little one is untruthful, inquire if, in his immediate circle of parents, nurses, teachers, and companions, there be not some one who is unconsciously serving him as a model. He may never have heard a direct untruth, but evasion, subterfuge, and concealment are brethren of lies, and so are the falsehoods of politeness.

It is folly for us to preach to him of the beauty of truth if he seldom sees it practiced; it is idle to point him to a road down which we never go ourselves; and before we give him any maxims on veracity let us ponder Emerson's terrible words, " How can I hear what you say, when what you *are* is thundering in my ears? "

Fear. Of all the motives to falsehood, fear seems to be the most potent and the commonest, begins earliest, and lasts longest.

Morbid fear of various kinds is a well-known symptom of neurasthenia, and is much more common among children than is ordinarily supposed. It need scarcely be considered in the case of a strong, healthy, mentally well-balanced child, but it is well to remember that there is such a thing as abnormal fear, and that in its various degrees it is a disease, and a disease of grave import.

In its normal state it is placed within us as a kind of necessary brake or safety-attachment; but note if, by your treatment of the child, you have not so aggravated the instinct that he is rendered absolutely incapable of truth-telling when under its influence. It is not probable that he stands in bodily terror of you, though cruelty to children is still to be found, even among the educated classes, but he fears your impatience, your passion, and your cutting rebuke. Perhaps he is by nature unusually sensitive, and a hasty word which you would hardly feel falls on him like the blow of a Russian knout. He deserves punishment, and probably knows it as well as you do, but your former judgments of him have been so disproportionately severe, and your uniform treatment so harsh, that you have added a thousand times to his natural equipment of fear, while you have lessened his courage in the same proportion. Tyranny always breeds deception; if you doubt it, you can turn to history for proof.

Desire for approval. Close on the heels of fear as a cause of falsehood comes the desire to please, which is almost a mania in some children. When normally developed, it is a useful passion which can safely be appealed to in educational training; but if unwisely treated, it may become a moral deformity.

It is one of the signs, when seen in excess, of a weak and sensitive nature which cannot be content unless its every word and action pleases those it loves. The child who possesses it hungers for approval, and, when truth is in question, withholds, colors, or distorts it, according as he fancies it will be most pleasing.

The falsehoods which grow from excessive desire to please are near akin to those which are prompted by the passion of emulation, and many of our school practices pander to both of them. Prize-giving and the system of ranking by credits are fruitful sources of deceit, and are as much to be condemned as excessive punishments.

Self-conceit. Egotism may be said to prompt another class of falsehoods which belong to later childhood (as well as to maturity), and which are generally brilliant fictions designed to surround the narrator with a blaze of glory. What Charles Reade calls "fluent, fertile, interesting, sonorous, prompt, audacious liars" belong to this class, and in early years it is not difficult to cure them by pricking the bubble of self-conceit.

Perhaps we may also include in this group the children who tell the lies of jealousy, for this surely has its root in egotism. These are they who can never learn of any feat of strength but they swear their father can do more, who never hear of any wonderful animal but they have it confined on their own premises, who never know of any interesting event but they want to persuade you that it has happened, is happening, or will happen to them.

Imagination. There is another so-called class of lies which are merely products of excessive imagination, and in little children these are often entirely misunderstood and mistreated. The child recounts many wonderful stories which never occurred, nor by any possibility could occur; but to tell him they are false, and punish him for them, as is often done, is to drive him into lying. Imagination is his dominant power, and what he sees happen in his dream-world, he gives as an actuality. His stage of mental development corresponds to the myth-age of the race, and by and by the age of reason will appear, when he will learn to separate and classify his mental impressions. In the meantime, while we listen to the young improvisatore, we can, by a little gentle comment, begin to make clear to him the difference between a "play" and a "truly story," and the place which each must occupy.

Pseudophobia. The student of childhood

also recognizes that lying may proceed from a mental obliquity, an absolute inability to see the truth clearly; but this is exceedingly uncommon, and constitutes a form of mental disease which the modern psychologists call *pseudophobia*.

While we are discussing these various forms of lies, let us note that there is frequently a period in the lives of young children when it is impossible to place much reliance on their statements; but this is commonly only a passing phase and need give us no serious anxiety, for it may be due as much to their imperfect grasp of language as to any other cause we have mentioned.

In the general treatment of falsehood it is wise to remember that Froebel believed inward clearness to proceed from outward order, and turn to the kindergarten as one of our aids to righteousness.

A continued series of exercises in exactness, accuracy, and measurement both of hand, eye, and brain; repeated observation that one false step at the beginning of work brings failure at every succeeding step; a clear conception of cause and effect, — all these are helps to truth-telling, and all these belong to the kindergarten.

Here, also, the imagination is guided, not suppressed, and new outlets for it found in the hearing of stories which in themselves may serve as a rebuke for falsehood, if the moral is woven into the very fabric of the tale.

Whether in home, kindergarten, or school, however, let us bear in mind that "the highest in the child is aroused only by example," and provide it not alone in ourselves, but in his nurses, teachers, and companions. We may also note, as we look back over the subject, that the great cause of untruth is weakness in one form or another, and therefore that it is incumbent upon us in the training of children to use every possible means to discourage self-indulgence, to cultivate self-respect, and to elevate the sense of personal honor. The whole nature of the weak and faltering human creature needs tonics, exercise, and strengthening baths, that it may run the race of life successfully. Not only is this true, but we must remember, in the words of one of the world's great teachers,[1] that "loyalty to truth is the most rare and difficult of human qualities, for such loyalty, as it grows in perfection, asks ever more and more of us, and sets before us a standard always rising higher and higher."

[1] Thomas Hughes.

"TELL ME A STORY"

"Since they be children, tell them of battles and kings, horses, devils, elephants, and angels, but omit not to tell them of love and such-like."

IF you follow the dusky track of the twilight as it tiptoes round the world, in land after land you and the twilight together will steal upon a little circle of children gathered about the knees of a story-teller. It may be where the stars are lighting their tapers in the deep sky above the desert sands; it may be by the flickering blubber lamp in the ice hut; by the firefly's torch in the green gloom of the tropic forest; where the feathery bamboos wave and the tea-plant blossoms white; or by the wigwam blaze on the lonely prairie.

Earth is circled with this vast company of story-tellers, nightly surrounded by their little ones, black, and white, and red, and brown, and yellow; their eager, upturned faces and eloquent voices all uttering the same plea, "Tell us a story, oh, tell us a story!"

So it was in the plains of Mamre when Abraham told tales of mighty kings and warriors of old to his dearly beloved Isaac; so it was in Egypt when the waiting-maids of the Princess poured their folk-lore into baby Moses' listening ears; so it was in the Garden of Eden probably, though really Eve must have been a person of such slight experience and scanty information that it is difficult to imagine what kind of stories she could have told to little Cain and Abel.

So it is, so it has been, so shall it always be, for the love of stories is inherent in the race. With some children a calm delight, with others an absolute passion, yet it exists in all in fair measure, and for ages past has been a great moral and educational agency. We of to-day, who live in a world of books, and who insist that our children shall be early taught to read, that they may the sooner, as Seguin wittily says, "cover the emptiness of their own minds with the patchwork of others"—we hardly realize, perhaps, the marvelous effect which a well-told story may produce upon the virgin mind and soul. It can but seem vastly more real and vital than the same thing seen in cold type on a printed page, and it has the added charm of look and movement and fitting gesture, in short, of dramatic expression. Before the days of book-knowledge, all the simple learning of the race was gained at the feet of the story-teller, who was the conserver of history and the repository of scientific fact. "The household story," as has been very well said, "was the earliest ethical study in the educational curriculum of the race;" and the extent to which it was used for this purpose may be measured by the strong moral sentiment pervading most of the nursery tales and childish legends which have come down to us from the olden time.

In these days of the thoughtful study of

childhood it has come to be pretty generally felt that educational training, to be successful, must be suited to child-nature, and that any exercise in which the normal, and for that matter the abnormal child takes unvarying delight must therefore, and on that account, be the one which may be made most serviceable to him. From the days of Eve the instinctive mother has ministered to the love of stories; but she cannot, in every case, be trusted to do so wisely until she knows the reasons for its existence and the purposes it may be made to serve.

What is the secret of the charm which story-telling has for the child? Is it not, first, perhaps, the fact that it interprets life — wonderful, mysterious, fascinating life — to him, and places in his hand a sort of telescope, through which he eagerly peers into the world across the threshold of his nursery? Is it not, again, that it addresses the imagination — his dominant power, his delight, his way of escape, that he may be able to bear the dullness, the denseness, the want of comprehension, of the grown-up world? Stories satisfy, too, his impatient feeling of justice, which the slow march of earthly events so often irritates, while they gratify his love of novelty and variety and his healthy curiosity. Froebel asserts that they arouse the inner life of the listener, that their flow carries him out of himself, and he thereby learns to measure himself more truly.

Fortunate, indeed, are we that what is so dear a delight may at the same time be used as an agent in mental and spiritual uplifting. Consider the story-teller, for instance, merely as the humble workman who rolls up the curtain that the drama of literature may begin. The curtain must be raised, else the play will remain a mystery, and an occasional half-heard voice only serve to tantalize the unfortunate audience.

Regarded in its proper light as the beginning of literature, the story assumes a more important position, and the duty at once becomes clear of selecting it wisely, that it may serve to lead to higher things. Because a child has a fresh, youthful appetite for tales of any kind, it does not follow that they will all give him equal nourishment. There are certain essentials which must always be considered in selecting a story. First, it must be true; by which I mean true when "ideally interpreted." The incidents need never have really occurred; indeed, some of the truest things have never yet happened, for "Fact at best," as George Macdonald says, "is but a garment of truth, which has ten thousand changes of raiment woven in the same loom." Then it must be suitable in length, for the art in this is like that of a letter — to leave off so that the hearer shall wish there was more of it. Should it not also keep in touch with the dominant interest of the day, if this be one appropriate to childhood? Indeed, if it is not appropriate, better seize the interest and turn it to nobler uses, for when the town is ringing with excitement over the outcome of a prize-fight it is idle to suppose your boy will be deaf to the echoes.

Why not take the occasion to introduce him to some of the grand figures of mythology, to the real heroes of history, or to recite some stirring ballad of doughty deeds which will make him feel what courage really is, and how a true knight uses his strength. So Mazzini advised mothers to do in the twilight hour, — to tell the children tales of great men who had worked and fought, and loved the people.

That the story should be clothed in well-chosen, fitting words, and narrated in as graceful a style as possible, goes without saying if you agree that the germs of literary taste begin to grow under its influence. I sincerely believe, however, that it is better to tell a story most clumsily and with a halting tongue than not to tell it at all. If it have a vital interest and hold a kernel of truth, the child will appropriate from it what he needs, in spite of its rude setting; for familiarity with good English and literary taste, valuable as they are, are not the only things developed by story-telling, — they are merely the beginning of the long category. We cannot teach a child by maxims, for instance (and I doubt if we can the adult until he has seen experience illustrate them); but pour the truth they hold into the mould of an attractive story, and watch the effect upon the mind. The tale is often asked for, if it is a really good one, and by and by the truth it enfolds takes root and grows, and will keep on growing though adverse winds of doctrine blow. By means of these narratives the child is confronted with actions and situations quite new to him, but upon which he must perforce pass unconscious judgment, and thus his discrimination is aroused and his ideals are strengthened. "Thus," as Mr. Hamilton Mabie says, "the individual life learns the lessons which universal life has learned, and pieces out its limited personal experience with the experience of humanity." You may spend hours, for instance, in moralizing to a child upon the beauty of unselfishness, and not produce a thousandth part of the effect which you might have made by telling him the story of gallant Philip Sidney and the cup of cold water given to one whose necessities were greater than his.

We must never neglect the purely imaginative tale when dealing with children, for, though we grown folk may live in a matter-of-fact world, the little ones are still by choice in the realm of fancy, and their place of residence must be considered when we select their literature. If imagination be the strongest element in the child's nature (and who can doubt it who really knows him), then it obviously needs wise guidance rather than repression. We may be sure the power is there for some good purpose, and that we ignore one of our highest possibilities for influence when we pass it by.

The fairy tale, with its simple, uninvolved plot, its transparent personages, its poetic atmosphere, and its hazy, indefinite time of action, is absolutely suited to children, who, as Mr. Howells says, " do not very distinctly know their dreams from their experiences, and live in a world where both project the same quality of shadow." Doubtless there are fairy tales entirely unfit for children, which have been perverted since they trickled long ago from the spring of universal myth; but the same objection may be made to absolute historic happenings, and the story-teller above all other persons needs constantly to exercise his judgment and his critical faculty.

Nor can there be any fear of telling the fairy tale too often when we reflect that the great stream of literature at our command has a host of branches, of which this is only one, and that " the earth is full of tales to him who listens."

There are the science stories, which may be made most valuable and interesting, and the patriotic ones, especially appropriate to the nation's holidays, which deal with the beginnings of history, and, by leading the child to admire, gradually bring him to love his country. Then there is perhaps now and then some tale which will develop sympathy with our kinsfolk the animals, or some wise little fable which will instruct as well as amuse. And why, in the name of all that is beautiful, do we confine ourselves so largely to prose when talking and reading to children? They are a hundred, a thousand times more susceptible than we to the linked sweetness of cadenced syllables, to the musical fall or martial swing of verse. I have seen many a stolid, lumpish child sit, breathing heavily, staring at the opposite wall, quite vacuous and unimpressed during the recital of an ordinary story, and yet if a line or two of poetry has fallen on his dull ear he has slowly turned toward the speaker, his glazed eye brightening, and animation transforming his whole expression. This he will do oftentimes, though the poem be almost entirely beyond his comprehension; and he will even rouse from his lethargy sufficiently to give a feeble encore, though he has never before been known to express any form of emotion.

One great drawback to the telling of stories, either in prose or verse, is that there are so few that can be bought ready-made, as it were. There seems to be a very general misconception on the part of authors as to what the child really likes, doubtless due to a mere bowing acquaintance with him, or to a superficial observation of the workings of his mind. Many collections of stories are *about* children rather than *for* them, and are much more appropriate for the adult in their careful delineation of character and accurate painting of emotions. Others are patiently written down to the child's level, as the saying goes, there being some general misunderstanding as to where that level is, and a failure on the part of the author to comprehend that it is frequently quite above his own head.

If one has had long experience with children, however, and knows them as well as one can know beings of another star, it is comparatively easy to adapt literature to their needs, to shorten here, to lengthen there, and generally to fit the garment to the wearer. Again, one may lack experience entirely and yet have an innate fitness for the work and an intuitive comprehension of and sympathy with childhood, which is in effect a kind of genius; and for these two classes of people the work of story-telling is easy.

But if one have neither natural adaptation nor experience, still I say, Tell the stories; tell the stories; a thousand times, tell the stories! You have no cold, unsympathetic audience to deal with; the child is helpful, receptive, warm, eager, friendly. His whole-hearted interest, his surprise, admiration, and wise comment, will spur you on to greater efforts, and when the story is concluded you will wonder which of you has been the greater gainer.

"THE AUTHENTIC" IN KINDERGARTEN TRAINING

"I serve you not, if you I follow,
Shadow-like, o'er hill and hollow."

A SERIES of discriminating essays by G. H. Lewes on the "Principles of Success in Literature" gives as one of these that of Authenticity. "What writers have seen and felt may not be new," he says, "it may not be intrinsically important; nevertheless, if authentic, it has its value, and a far greater value than anything reported by them at second hand. We cannot demand from every man that he have unusual depth of insight or exceptional experiences; but we demand of him that he give us of his best, and his best cannot be another's. The facts seen through the vision of another, reported on the witness of another, may be true, but the reporter cannot vouch for them. Let the original observer speak for himself. Otherwise only rumors are set afloat."

Is not this equally true in all art, whether it be painting, sculpture, literature, or education? Of what use the attempt to paint a composition never seen by one's self with eye of flesh, or eye of spirit, but merely selected as a taking subject? Of what avail to spend months of time and labor in carving a statue, the ideal for which never existed in one's own brain, which is the half-assimilated fruit of another's suggestion and which when completed must lack the strength of sincerity? A landsman who scarcely knew the rig of one ship from another would make a poor figure at writing a novel of the sea, and should he attempt to do so because sea stories happened to be popular, he would inevitably make a failure because his narrative was not the outcome of personal experience. How could he describe the seethe of the foam, the sparkling roll of the wave, the tang of the salt air, the song of the wind in the sails, the dancing, springing, buoyant motion, if he had never been at sea, but gathered his data from the Encyclopædia and wrote his tale in a garret chamber?

Who would attempt to write a poem dealing with the dark intrigues, the miseries, the complications, the imbroglios, of life in a palace of the Orient, if he received his information at second hand from a man who had once been behind the scenes? If a minister of the gospel acknowledged that he knew nothing personally of the holy mysteries he was discussing, but had the facts from his father in whose experience he believed, we should scorn to listen to his idle words.

It is the authentic which is of value, it is the report at first hand, the painting which bears the mark of personality, the statue which shows the touch of the individual, the poem, the novel, the essay, fresh, original, glowing with conviction, and valuable because the old facts, ideas, and thoughts have been passed through a new mind, and have come forth stamped with a new image.

A commentary on a commentary of the Holy Scriptures never yet convinced the unbeliever of the truths of righteousness; notes on a French translation of a German rendering of Shakespeare's plays would hardly succeed in impressing the reader with the genius of the great dramatist; and if we take the subject into the realm of education, we shall find that the teaching which is the product of our own convictions is the only one which is of value. One must write, paint, carve, act, think, speak, teach, in accordance with one's own temperament, one's own character and individuality. Bright, breezy, Miss So-and-So may be delightful when she gives her lessons and exercises in her own vivacious manner, but it does not follow that Miss Such-an-One with her serene, reflective temperament could teach in any such manner, even though Miss So-and-So finds it most successful. Mr. Blank's pamphlet of devices in number-teaching is most vigorous and helpful; Mr. Dash acknowledges this, he gets many valuable hints from it, but he knows that he cannot teach number in that way. He has learned, as Emerson says, that the inventor did it because it was natural to him, but for any one else to do merely what he has done is the veriest of slavish servitude, out of which nothing good can come.

In all education, and in kindergarten education in particular, there is too much using of John Brown's notes on John Smith's commentary on John Jones's translation of the original.

We accept one person's experience in art-teaching, another's views on discipline, another's method of musical instruction, still another's way of imparting the elements of science, until our work is a thing of shreds and patches, caught together here and there with a thread of our own personality. Not that all these things were not of value to the minds in which they grew and to which they were adapted; not that we cannot gain much from reading and observation; but that we must learn to discover in each new suggestion the valuable principle it contains, and retain and assimilate that, not the garb in which it was clothed.

Froebel himself gives the kindergartner repeated warnings on the dangers of discipleship, saying, " Again, a life whose ideal value has been perfectly established in experience never aims to serve as a model in its form, but only in its essence, — in its spirit. It is the greatest mistake to suppose that spiritual human perfection can serve as a model in its form. This accounts for the common experience, that the taking of such external manifestations of perfection as examples, instead of elevating mankind, checks — nay, represses its development."

Montaigne speaks of the " indiscreet scribblers " of his time, who laboriously quote whole pages from ancient authors " with a design by that means to illustrate their own writings;" but, he says, this "infinite dissimilitude of ornaments renders the complexion of their own compositions so pale, sallow, and deformed that they lose much more than they get."

The further the principle of imitation, of feeble following after, is continued, the more noteworthy are its evil effects. It is like a child's first writing-copy, which he laboriously traces down the slate. He looks each time at the last line he wrote, not at the model at the top, and so it happens that the fourth line has already lost much of its resemblance to the original and is deciphered only with difficulty, while the line at the bottom is a succession of meaningless strokes.

Kindergarten training is often like the writing on the slate, carried out with patient labor, but, ah, how woefully different from the original it follows! And when this imitation is followed by another imitation, then indeed it becomes like the last row on the slate, absolutely meaningless, had one not seen the model somewhere.

Miss A. perhaps is a most successful kindergartner. She brings a "pair of fresh eyes" to her work; she is original, independent, a student, and a thinker. Her success is spread abroad, her kindergarten is visited and admired. By and by some one comes and begs that Miss A. will give her a course of kindergarten training. Miss A. is modest, has never thought of such a thing, and declines the honor, but other persons come, and still others, and ultimately she is persuaded to undertake a class. She does the work with her might; she studies and she thinks. She makes mistakes, for she is a woman, therefore human; but the interpretations of Froebel which she gives are the outcome of her own thought and experience and study; her instruction is authentic; it is fresh, suggestive; it is the result of conviction. Her "originality grows by progressive deepening of insight into the causes and motives of the thing imitated, and with the ascending comprehension of means and purposes." Her work succeeds as a matter of course, and her first class leaves her sheltering wing, filled with enthusiasm and deeply convinced of the sacred nature of the duties they have undertaken. Miss B. is one of their number, and after a few years' experience she concludes to begin training work, not perhaps from any such pressure of public opinion as influenced Miss A., but because she honestly thinks she is fitted for it. But Miss B. is not a thinker; she uses Miss A.'s commentaries, confident that there can be nothing better. She remembers how strongly they stirred her growing spirit, but forgets that they can never be delivered at second hand with the same enthusiasm and conviction, forgets also, or has never learned, that "imitation can never go above its level" and that "the imitator dooms himself to hopeless mediocrity from the very outset." She uses all Miss A.'s practical methods, most of which fit her but poorly, and, because she does not feed the flame of originality and independence which God gave to her, it smoulders down and out into dead, gray ashes. She is earnest, she is conscientious, but she is killing the spirit with the letter. She might have done good work had she developed her own power, her own gifts, but as she merely repeats the opinions of another, she fails to impress her class with the holiness of the ground on which they tread.

Close upon Miss B.'s heels follows Miss C., who is probably the least hopeful member of the class, and who begins to teach others long before she has digested her experience as a student.

With lightning rapidity Miss D. arrives upon the scene. Introduced to kindergarten work by Miss C., she naturally fails to look upon it in a serious light. She sees in it an agreeable and easy way of earning a livelihood, and immediately seeks for others around whom she can wreathe her octopus arms, and to whom she can impart the tricks of the trade.

Now indeed is the writing blurred and meaningless; but Miss E. turns the slate over and begins work on the other side, and it is probable that in remote mountain villages and solitary hamlets her pupils, Misses F., G., H., I., J., and K., are now buying slate-pencils and preparing to write.

The undoubted fact has not here been touched upon that Miss A. frequently has a pupil a hundred times more gifted than herself. Once taught to use her eagle wings, she soars to regions far beyond her teacher's reach, and her flight is a swift onward rush of power, strength, and inspiration.

Nor can it be denied that Miss B., who is, after all, careful, conscientious, and painstaking, succeeds now and then in giving the key of the universe to some eager soul who uses it aright and unlocks for herself and others the stores of wisdom that lie hidden therein.

But we may be assured, with all assurance, that Misses C., D., and E. have never helped one struggling life, but have only falsified and held up to scorn an educational idea which, when properly interpreted, is one of truth, beauty, and righteousness.

Why may we not establish a Pre-Raphaelite Brotherhood of Kindergartners, and, casting aside all the traditions, the prejudices, the rumors, the hearsay evidence in regard to the Froebelian principles, go back to the fountain-head and once again drink deeply there?

In the old days before Raphael, each artist, musing in his solitary cloister, or pacing the narrow streets of his walled city, developed his powers in quiet and in silence, and without influence laid upon him from without. If he sang, or painted, or carved, it was but the flowering of his powers of expression, which had slowly grown and budded without artificial stimulus. Whatever the character of the creation, it must have been authentic, for the artist had only himself to imitate.

In our complex, crowded modern life such work is no longer possible; we must touch others and be influenced by them; we must " do good and communicate," but whenever the kindergartner writes and speaks on the principles of Froebel, or seeks to impart them to others, let her assure herself that she does it with authenticity, that her interpretations, whatever they may be, are her own, the fruit of her study and experience, and therefore entitled to consideration.

We have perfected many of the details of Froebel's system, and shall perfect more; we have pruned in one place, have added in another, and have discarded some features which no longer seemed essential; but we have not yet improved upon the principles of the discoverer.

A devoted study of those principles, carried on sometimes without the aid of commentators or commentaries, a voyage on our own account into the realms of truth, will ever give us fresh stores of enthusiasm and inspiration.

THE GOSPEL OF WORK

"Properly thou hast no other knowledge but what thou hast got by working."

CARLYLE concludes his chapter on the "Everlasting Yea" with the words: "Produce! Produce! Were it but the pitifulest infinitesimal fraction of a Product, produce it in God's name! 'T is the utmost thou hast in thee; out with it! Get leave to work in this world,— 't is the best you get at all; for God in cursing gives us better gifts than men in benediction. God says 'Sweat for foreheads,' men say 'Crowns;' and so we are crowned,— ay! gashed, by some tormenting circle of steel which snaps with a secret spring. Get work. Be sure 't is better than what you work to get."

The uplifting of labor — it is a common thought and phrase to-day — depends largely on the uplifting of the laborer, that is, upon qualifying him for service that shall ennoble, as every craft exercising thought, intelligence, and skill necessarily tends to do. Not long ago a very forcible and searching address upon this topic was made before a Charity Conference by a plain, practical business man who was not too plain, and was yet sufficiently practical, to see the subject in a comprehensive way, and to discover among other things how absolutely the whole spirit of kindergarten work is in line with the best thought of the day upon the question.

The host of drudges, as Carlyle calls them, can now do only drudgery; so, in servile toil life wears itself away, and the ranks of the feeble, the dull, the vicious, the diseased, the criminal, are constantly replenished.

Our business man remarked, among other things, — and all who deal with the problem of want in our great cities know that he was right, — that the reason the very poor are unable to secure work above drudgery is largely because they are fit for nothing better, and thus they drag down labor of every grade, and heavily clog the wheels of the social mechanism. This fact has long been so keenly felt by thinking people that attention has for some time past been directed to the necessity of the education of labor, and art schools, schools of design, manual training-schools, and even the common schools in some of their later features have begun to supply the need.

Valuable as all these educational institutions are, they yet lack much, not only in that they are sporadic, rather than universal, — for a few children, not for all, — but in that they lack a proper foundation. They come much too late in the lives of most young persons submitted to their influence to do the good they might have done under happier circumstances, for probably, in too many cases, muscles have become stiff and hands awkward, while æsthetic taste is past the best formative period, and mental habits, difficult to change, have already been partially fixed.

We who believe in the kindergarten consider that if labor is to be successfully raised, the lever must be pushed well under at the very bottom of the weight, and then the force applied, and we also believe that Froebel has given us the proper implement for the task, and shown us how to use it. It seems to us in our experience among little children that the kindergarten is the greatest of all instrumentalities for producing originative, thoughtful labor, and we note that it sometimes literally seems to make, out of most unpromising material, too, judgment, quick sight, subtle touch, the sense of beauty, and creative ability, — all powers which, when once developed, forever lift manual labor above the level of mere mechanical toil.

The following verse is written above the doors of the St. Louis Manual Training-School : —

> "Hail to the skillful, cunning hand!
> Hail to the cultured mind!
> Contending for the world's command,
> Here let them be combined!"

The same words might fitly be set over the entrance to every good kindergarten, although another line,—

"Hail to the loving, helpful heart!"

would really be needed to make the verse fully comprehensive of our purposes.

Laying aside for a time the distinctive and special value of the kind of work given in the kindergarten and its value as early manual training, we cannot fail to see its general bearing upon the formation of habits of industry.

If the kindergartner has the art to provide the right conditions for their growth, the virtues of neatness, order, economy, and carefulness flourish with us as in their native air.

The normal child is never unhappy if he has sufficient and suitable occupation, for to be idle is against the very constitution of his nature. In the kindergarten he is always busy and therefore, generally speaking, always contented and joyous. The striking peculiarity of the good kindergarten — one that never fails to impress the novice and the casual visitor, as well as those grown old in the service — is the atmosphere of happiness diffused throughout the room. It is exceptional to see a child among the company who is anything but absorbed and happy in his work, and the removal of that work is one of the severest penalties that can be inflicted upon the small evil-doer.

Habits of obedience to law must carefully be cultivated before the children can be persuaded cheerfully to give up their occupation, whatever it may be, at the expiration of the short work-period, and at Christmas time, or other festival season, the teacher must constantly be on the alert, lest the spirit of industry exceed its proper limits and become a delirium. Under wise guidance, the child trained according to Froebel becomes not only industrious, but self-helpful also, and a sure test of the fitness of the kindergartner for her vocation is whether or not her pupil comes up to this

THE GOSPEL OF WORK 133

standard. If she has succeeded, the child is not only busy and happy under her influence, but busy, happy, and resourceful at home, a famous mother's-helper, originator of delightful games, and source of fascinating employment to lesser ones of the flock.

Froebel had no mind, however, that his gospel of work should be preached in the kindergarten only, for he notes in all his writings, and particularly in "The Education of Man," the instinctive (and sometimes exceedingly troublesome) desire of the child to extend his feeble help to whatever household occupation may be going on, and he urges parents, by all that they hold sacred in the nature of that child, and by all their hopes for his future, to cherish this desire, to afford opportunities for its gratification, lest once suppressed it arise no more. To do. this, to think of small ways in which a small person may be helpful, or at least think he is helpful; to resist the temptation to send him into the garden or into the nursery — anywhere out of the way, when household work is going on — often costs great pains and trouble, which is only to be cheerfully borne by taking a long, refreshing look into the future and thinking of the immense labor thereby saved at the other end of the line. Alas, it is so difficult to live *with* the children and resist the temptation to substitute some other preposition for that small, significant word.

There is still another phase of the gospel of work as preached by Froebel, — one much more technical, quite distinct from the habit of cheerful occupation I have dwelt upon, and more closely related, perhaps, to the uplifting of labor.

It is probably conceded by every one who has taken thought of the matter at all, that manual skill is acquired to a considerable extent in the kindergarten, notwithstanding the youth of the pupils, and that it is a valuable acquisition nobody appears to doubt, though it would be interesting to discover for what reasons it is so considered. The answers to the question would of course be many and varied, according as the subject is seen from this or that standpoint. One person would say, possibly: "These children have hands, and many of them will be dependent upon the use of them for support; therefore train them in the industries, the members of the poorer classes particularly."

Such reasoning is sufficiently good, perhaps, as far as it goes, though the poor of this year may be the rich of fifteen years to come, and the rich of to-day may be, by and by, among the poorest.

Others say: "Idle fingers are the devil's tools. The children's hands will be employed in any case, and if we do not furnish useful occupation, mischief will be the alternative."

Very true, we answer, although not so far-reaching a view of the question as might be desired.

Still another person might reply, and he

would be right, we believe: "These little children have hands capable of becoming active, powerful instruments of an active, intelligent, self-determining will; therefore, in order that the human creature be conscious of his capabilities in all directions, and be able to express his ideas in other ways than by words alone, the hands must be trained, and the best tangible results will follow." But these tangible results are only secondary, it must be understood. It is the higher meaning of labor which we believe to be the most valuable acquisition to children. It is as Alice Wellington Rollins said: "We are really to aim at results only as a dog aims at catching the stick his master has thrown for him. He does not care for the stick; what he likes is the running."

Each tangible result of kindergarten work or action is only a symbol of something more valuable which the child has acquired in doing it. The finished product is not half so much a matter of pride as the consciousness of power to create, for the kindergarten is not, and was never intended to be, an infant industrial school, although we believe that it forms a basis for a rational system of education from which work is not excluded.

Dr. W. N. Hailmann says: "The training of the hand is an essential need of education, because —

"1. The hand is the instrument by which man controls, modifies, and prepares surroundings for use.

"2. Because the hand is the medium by which the *internal* (mind) is brought into living, actual connection with the *external* (matter).

"3. Because the hand is the organ of the plastic expression of ideas."

The recognition of practical activity as an integral part of education is one of the salient truths of Froebel's system. Many educators had previously attached value to manual exercise and handicraft of various kinds, but rather as parts of physical training and technical preparation for life, especially among the poorer classes; but with

Froebel all outward training had an inward correlative: some mental faculty was always to be consciously brought into play to be strengthened and directed aright, while the limbs were gaining dexterity and vigor.

He did not, in fact, value manual work for the sake merely of making a better workman, but for the sake of making a more complete human being.

While the kindergarten trains the hands of little children to express their thoughts and fancies skillfully, and, so far as their capabilities go, with accuracy, it trains with equal care their powers of language as another means of expression. The kindergarten child may be better prepared than others for industrial pursuits, but he is also, we believe, better prepared for all future life, whatever it may be, inasmuch as his powers and faculties have received equal and harmonious training.

Our system of public instruction has, up to the present, generally begun with the abstract, with which it should close, and this procedure is obviously in the highest degree irrational, particularly for the mass of the people whose task in later life is work that must be productive. Any system of education which leaves the hand entirely out of the question must therefore be grievously in error, although manual training must never be suffered to supersede in any way the rightful claims of mental training. The first educational task is to make the child acquainted with the things of the material world which constitute the basis of the abstract, for, as Froebel says, "the A B C of things must precede the A B C of words, and give to the words their true foundations." Knowledge of concrete things can only be gained by handling them, and the formation and transformation of material is therefore for children the best mode of gaining this knowledge. Froebel's occupations offer all possible facilities for this experimentation, and give the activity which is necessary to childish powers, that they may not be lost for want of use. We place much greater stress upon fertility of invention in all our work than upon perfection of execution, which indeed is hardly possible or to be desired at this early age. There is no carelessness, it must be understood; everything must be done, if not absolutely well, at least as well as the child can do it, but what we consider the important matter is "not so much that he shall do the right thing, as that he shall like doing the right thing."

All the kindergarten exercises are closely related one to the other, and the work-materials in every case supplement and translate one another, for Froebel's great hope for education is in unification of thought and deed and life. The kindergarten is intended to be an organic whole, and Froebel pleads for unification of thought and unification of life by means of the unification of the materials of thought and unification of the preparation for life. An all-sided connectedness gives an interest, a novelty, an intelligibility to school work that nothing else can give, and to this may be attributed the fact already noted, that there are surprisingly few sulky, indifferent, languid children in good kindergartens.

"Life, action, and knowledge were to Froebel the three notes of one harmonious chord," and he says, therefore, "God made every child with hands as well as head, and if the brain depends upon systematic training for its power, so does the hand, and so does the moral sense. The individual is bereft of power in proportion as any faculty is left untrained, and thus the will of God is in so far left unfulfilled." He believed in the cultivation of the habit of work as a resource and as a blessing, but in so educating the worker in the totality of his powers from his earliest days, by training his hands, by cultivating his senses, by furnishing him with employment suited to develop the æsthetic faculties, that his labor would be no longer mechanical toil, but original, creative production valuable to the world, because stamped with the image of a new individuality. This is, in brief, the view of the kindergarten as to the harmonious development of the powers of each human being, its conception of the training which must be given if he is to take his place in the world as an active, useful member of society.

We do not claim, however, that the kindergarten has said the last word on the subject, that it has reached the *ultima thule* of educational progress, for we realize that it has but set out in the right direction. Froebel himself went no further than modestly to say, after half a century of study, observation, and experiment, "This is, in my judgment, *about* the way children should be trained."

THE BROTHERHOOD OF SAINT TUMBLER

"Happy must be his heart and mind
Whose task it is to help his kind."

THERE is a twelfth century church legend which, for the good of humanity, should be issued in cheap tract form in all known languages and distributed to every grown person of both sexes, in this and other countries. Had I my way, men should stand on street corners in all towns and cities, pressing these pamphlets upon each passer-by; and mounted colporteurs should gallop over every land, urging their swift steeds through rocky mountain defile and dry and desolate waste, that no poor hut, sequestered hamlet, or outlying homestead might be forgotten in the general distribution.

More than this, I would, could I find a few faithful followers, engage to robe myself as a minstrel, and with my lute wander the world over, telling the tale in every spot where an audience of two persons could be gathered together. These two, or half of them, at least, I should hope straightway to enroll into a general association, to be known as the Brotherhood of Saint Tumbler, — a devoted band ready to lay down life itself for its beliefs, and pledged to expound them throughout the world. For myself, as the promoter of the order, and therefore presumably most conversant with its principles, I should reserve a special field, now white for the harvest, — say in Russia, Germany, and the Scandinavian countries, and as I swept my lute in the principal marts of traffic, this would be, in brief, and divested of the minstrel's arts, the substance of my tale.

. . . .

Once upon a time, — long ago, God knows, for those were other days and other people, — there dwelt afar in France a strolling mountebank, a juggler, a circus dancer, a tumbler, — what you will, — who made his living among the kindly country folk by the various tricks of his calling. He was a simple, merry fellow, who danced and tumbled for pure joy of life and delight in the world, and wherever he went, a trail of song and laughter followed him. Children shrieked with delight and toddled into the street, clapping their fat hands when they saw his bright dress and his glittering spangles, and staid fathers stopped their work, and mothers ran with babies to the doors, that they might catch the sparkle of his eyes and the gleam of the white teeth behind the laughing lips, as he tumbled in the dust. His merry heart made a cheerful countenance in all who saw him; his presence was a continual feast, and the few coppers men threw him for his capers would have been well spent had they been gold pieces.

Now this poor tumbler had a heart full of tender faith and reverence, and seeing how valuable men deemed the simple talents God had given him, he resolved to offer them up in thanksgiving to the source from whence they came. So he sought out an ancient monastery, and being admitted there as one of the ministering brothers, resolved to spend the remainder of his life in worship of the Queen of Heaven.

But now, alas, for the first time he felt his inferiority, for while priests, deacons, and sub-deacons all might engage in the religious services, he, ignorant of books or letters, had no part among them. He wandered disconsolate through the old gray building, and at last in a desolate crypt found a forgotten altar and a dusty image of the Virgin set upon it.

Here was an opportunity for service, alone and unseen, free from the criticism of his learned fellows; what could he do here to pleasure the Blessed Lady? Ah, he knew nothing save the tricks of his trade, but sweet mothers and innocent little ones had always smiled upon them, and why should not the ever holy Mother, friend of children, accept them, smiling also, if he but performed them with the full perfection of his art? So he threw his robe upon the damp stones, and in the silent dusk, before the deserted altar, began his leaps, his contortions, and his somersaults with all the ardor of religious enthusiasm.

Day after day, in these incongruous surroundings, the strange, silent, grotesque service was continued, until the poor tumbler, half fainting with exhaustion, fancied at last that he saw the parted lips of the Virgin smiling upon him. Overcome by fatigue and emotion, he sank into a deathlike swoon, and after a long interval, being missed by the brethren, was finally tracked to the lonely altar. They entered eagerly, tapers in hand, but their lights were dimmed by the moonlike radiance that overbrimmed the crypt, for, as they stood in awe and wonder, above the ignorant mountebank hovered the Blessed Queen of Heaven herself, and a sky full of glorious angels.

. . . .

Now my hope would be that if I played my lute with art, if I told my tale with what grace God had given me, and at least with all the ardor of Blessed Saint Tumbler himself, that, as its last words left my lips, certain persons would force themselves through the crowd, trembling with eagerness to be sworn into the order. I should receive them gladly, but I should know from their ready acceptance of the doctrine that they had probably practiced it unwittingly from their youth up, and while I sent them away at once as missionaries, I should devote all my eloquence to the Doubting Thomases among the crowd, who greatly needing the benefits of the order themselves, yet were skeptical of its value to the world.

I should lay aside my lute, and we would reason together, and these are some of the things I should probably say, though they would scarcely be so didactic in form as they here appear.

We talk a great deal about the wisdom

of Solomon, my friends, but I wonder if we have any idea of how many and what sensible things he had to say upon the value of cheerfulness. The "Mirth Cure," recently advocated by some French physicians, is really neither so novel nor so original as the critics would have us think, for it is thousands of years since the great king of Israel declared that a merry heart doeth good like a medicine. Nor is Solomon the only famous writer who upholds the Mirth Cure, for Horace and Milton and Cervantes and Shakespeare, especially Shakespeare, have scores of wise and brilliant things to say about that "merriment which bars a thousand harms and lengthens life." That this statement in regard to merriment is true to scientific fact, and not merely a hazy poetic generality, is provable enough, and any one of us could doubtless furnish a dozen instances in point, were such required to support the argument. It is possible that some of the marvelous healing adduced by the mental scientists is near akin to that performed by the Mirth Cure, for the peculiar beliefs of these devoted people certainly seem to produce in them a marked serenity and joyousness of disposition, beautiful to see in an anxious and troubled world. And again, still looking at the subject from the standpoint of self, tomes might be written on the value of cheerfulness to the human mind, of the healthy glow it diffuses over thought, of the sweet sanity of contemplation it makes possible, of the sunny mental tone it engenders, vigorously shining away clouds of depression and trouble that threaten permanent injury to the sensitive climate of the brain.

But can we think of the subject from the standpoint of self alone? Is it not altruistic in its very nature? Was not Dryden quite right when he said: —

> "Nature, in zeal for human amity,
> Denies or damps an undivided joy;
> Joy is an import; joy is an exchange;
> Joy flies monopolists; joy calls for two."

Can a real gayety of heart, one that

wells up from within, be pent in one's own breast? Must it not gush out, like the spring itself, for the refreshing of every wayfarer?

Is it not true, in Stevenson's words, — he to whom joy was a religion, — that by being happy we sow anonymous benefits upon the world, which remain unknown even to ourselves? That gallant spirit, frail, suffering, weighted with pain and weakness, and yet making so brave a fight, presenting to the world so serene and undaunted a front, furnishes a fit text indeed from which to preach a sermon on cheerfulness, — one which should put to shame the grumbler and the misanthrope.

Is not joy, — for these are all merely conversational suggestions, to be filled out by the hearer, — is not joy infectious and contagious also? Think of a skylark caroling up into the mist, of the fire-glow on a rainy day, or better still, of a baby's smile and the light that comes into every face as, carried through a crowded car, the sunny glance shines backward over the mother's shoulder. It is one of the commonest incidents of every-day life, this, for babies are common enough, and fortunately, on their bright faces, smiles are equally so. It is obvious that this spontaneity of joy must decrease with age and experience and trouble and knowledge of the heavy mysteries of life, but need its sources dry away altogether, or is there not some fount from which they may be replenished?

He is fortunate to-day who holds the power to make people laugh, if only they laugh at wholesome things and thoughts. We can always find something to weep for, without overmuch labor, but cause for merriment must frequently be sought outside ourselves and with difficulty. He who looks for it in the literature of the day, however, will often have his labor for his pains, for a strain of morbidity and sadness breathes through much of it, and it is only necessary to bring many a so-called cheerful book to the test of the sick-room to discover how lamentably it comes short of its reputation. It is so easy to win a name for brilliancy by writing with the pen of the cynic; the pessimist can be so original at such slight expense that it is the less wonder that the style is so popular a one. It is difficult to be witty without being sarcastic, and difficult to be funny except at other people's expense. The disagreeable things are always sharpest and most trenchant, — else, why does Polly remember the "swear-words" so easily?

And here one takes thought of the children again, who cannot indeed be long out of mind in such a book as this. There are no words, it seems to me, that can fitly estimate the worth to them of a companionship which is full of this buoyancy, this light-heartedness, this simple gayety. An eminent speaker on education has lately said that in the days to come, no cynic, pessimist, or morbid person will ever be given a teacher's appointment, and all lovers of children will ardently hope for the fulfillment of the prophecy. These little ones are too sensitive, too impressionable, to be exposed to the influence of melancholy, which, like the chill darkness of a cellar, inevitably blanches and blights every fresh bud of mind and soul. We know well enough that sunshine is an absolute necessity of growth, but we sometimes forget that moral and mental sunshine are included in this essential.

Happiness in childhood, and this is not sentimentality, but the dictum of the scientist, is fundamentally necessary to development. Pains and fears and anxieties all repress growth, say our modern psychologists, and it has been clearly proved that nervous shocks, great griefs, distresses of any kind, suspend some of the vital processes for a time.

It has been shown by careful medical observations that the physical results of depressing emotions are similar to those caused by bodily accidents, fatigue, chill, partial starvation, and loss of blood. Birds, moles, and dogs, which apparently died in consequence of capture, and from conditions that correspond in human beings to acute nostalgia and "broken heart," were examined after death as to the condition of their internal organs. Nutrition of the tissues had been interfered with, and the substance proper of various vital organs had undergone the same kind of degeneration as that brought about by phosphorus, or the germs of infectious disease. The poisons of grief, of sorrow, of fear, of misery are more than names.[1]

Whatever may be said of the mysterious ministry of pain, of the value of sorrow as a discipline in maturity, we may be assured that such a discipline is not for childhood, which needs a free and joyous atmosphere where it may grow and expand all its possibilities. If it be wrapped about with misery and gloom, the growth of brain will be slow and that of body much impaired.

We who have grown older can live, and

[1] *Medical Record.*

must live oftentimes, under dark clouds and in a bleak environment, but it must not be forgotten that we have come to our full stature, and, like the deep-rooted forest tree, make less of chilling frost, of ice and snow and tempest, than does the budding rose-bush in the garden.

Ah, but this is all a matter of temperament, you say. He who is born cheerful will remain cheerful; but he who comes into the world under an unlucky star must e'en remain so, and bewail his fate.

Some part of this feeling is doubtless rooted in truth, just as there is no question that certain virtues are more easily practiced than others by certain natures, and some can with difficulty be practiced at all. Part of the feeling is true, but how much of it? If as we are born so must we die, if our spots are as unchangeable as the leopard's own, then the whole scheme of the universe is wrong, and we are the blackest detail in the plan. But to believe this is to disbelieve everything else, and that in itself is madness. . . .

Good friends, my plea is ended; let who will speak now.

Ho, ye! stand forward, all who would join the Brotherhood of Saint Tumbler!

THE KINDERGARTEN IN NEIGHBORHOOD WORK

"This bond of neighborhood is, after all, one of the most human — yea, of the most divine — of all bonds. Every man you meet is your brother, and must be, for good or for evil."

IN these days of social settlements, of neighborhood guilds, of friendly aid houses, of all wholesome, helpful organizations based on the brotherhood of man, the free kindergartens feel a pardonable pride as they reflect that they have been in and of this work from the beginning. The kindergarten is as yet but a grain of mustard seed which has scarcely begun to sprout; but it is rooted in all good things, it is related to all forward movements, and these facts assure us that it is destined to grow until, as Froebel saw it in prophetic vision, it becometh a tree, so that the birds of the air come and lodge in the branches thereof.

The development of the child in his three-fold relations with nature, with God, and with mankind is the first article in the kindergarten creed, and, as the little one is led to feel the last relationship, all neighborhood life is touched upon.

There is no other educational system which has this social basis, and therefore no other which is so well adapted to serve as a foundation for all schemes of social regeneration. The age of the children is such that the teacher must naturally regard them with a tender and protective feeling, and this attitude of mind being quickly felt and appreciated by the mother, the two women join hands in love for the little one, and the first links in the chain are welded together. To and fro, between home and school, the children go, blessed little messengers of good will; and, when the kindergartner calls to see the mother or the mother comes to advise with the kindergartner, they are not strangers, though they may never have met before, for so much has been reported about the one to the other that they seem quite like old friends. The ideal leader of the free kindergarten knows well every one of the families whose children are in her care; she has visited every home in a friendly way, and thus gained an understanding of the heredity of the child and his environment, which she could have obtained in no other manner. Seeing her genuine interest in the little one, her opinion of his abilities, her joy in his achievements, the parents learn to value him still more, and are drawn nearer together by their pride and love.

Thus the neighborhood work begins, and to show how it has broadened out from thence in a certain institution in the far West will be to show what is and must be the inevitable effect everywhere of Froebel's principles as applied to community life.

In the first place, then, the babies who spend the years from three to six in close companionship with the kindergartner become dear, familiar friends, who will not and cannot be shaken off when they have graduated into the public schools. They return to bring their little brothers and sisters; they drop in to learn how the younglings are getting on; they call often to see if they may do errands or give any sort of assistance; they spend all possible holidays in the charmed atmosphere, and generally cling to the place like a devoted heap of iron filings to a very powerful magnet. What can be done with this army of devoted followers? thought the kindergartners in that Western institution long ago; is there not some useful and pleasant work that we can give them?

The demand was urgent, and the supply, being eagerly looked for, did not fail in coming. The housekeeper's class, or kitchen garden, originated by Miss Emily Huntington, of the Wilson Industrial School for Girls (New York), was described to the teachers, and they immediately formed a class, on the same lines, for girls from nine to fifteen years. This, with its simple instruction in household duties, its pleasant suggestions as to the best ways of washing and ironing, sweeping, dusting, and table-setting, brought them again in touch with the home, and another band of messengers sped to and fro on their kindly errands.

But here were the boy graduates, a little shyer about calling to offer their services, but covering the steps and even ornamenting the fences after school-hours, and, through want of occupation, often making themselves rather troublesome visitors. A generous friend came to their rescue, and four years ago the Boys' Free Library was opened on the ground floor of the building. Here, in bright, pleasant surroundings, from two to six o'clock every afternoon, from fifty to sixty of the neighborhood boys are welcomed and provided with books, magazines, and quiet games.

Now the hands of the teachers were clasped in those of the little children and of the older boys and girls, and they were necessarily in close relation with the home.

But they wanted to do more for the mothers — some of them so patient and hardworking, so sweet and good; others so vicious and hardened, and ignorant and dull. So the kindergartners asked these needy women to come to them regularly for friendly chats about the children, for explanation of Froebel's work-materials and the purpose of the songs and games, for bits of talk about home matters and simple addresses on such important subjects as children's diseases and remedies, children's food and clothing, methods of discipline, etc. These mothers' meetings were brightened with tea, and music, and conversation, and became a regular and most valuable feature of the institution work.

The last year has seen two more very important additions to the social life of the neighborhood, — the opening of the Library on two evenings a week for boys and young men at work by day, and the giving up of the rooms on Saturday afternoons to the girls, who have been provided with cases of books especially suited to their needs.

Now the circle is almost complete, the kindergartners are in close relation with the little children, the boys and girls, the mothers and homes of the neighborhood, and their next outward reach must be toward the fathers, whom they have only touched as yet by proxy, as it were.

Over three hundred and fifty human beings, of all ages, go in and out every week through the hospitable doors of this institution; and in many cases the workers hope — nay, they *know* — that what is gained under that roof is a blessing to the entire neighborhood.

It is but a little piece of the world's work, they realize; they might have reached out further had they had more money, they might have done better had they been wiser, they might have done more nobly had they seen more clearly; but they have done what they could, and they have few fears for the future. And so, —

"Here's to the Cause, and the years that have passed!
Here's to the Cause — it will triumph at last!
The End shall illumine the hearts that have braved
All the years and the fears, that the Cause might be
    saved.
And though what we hoped for, and darkly have groped
    for,
Come not in the manner we prayed that it should,
We shall gladly confess it, and the Cause, may God
    bless it!
Shall find us all worthy who did what we could!"

The Riverside Press
CAMBRIDGE, MASSACHUSETTS, U. S. A.
ELECTROTYPED AND PRINTED BY
H. O. HOUGHTON AND CO.

www.ingramcontent.com/pod-product-compliance
Lightning Source LLC
Chambersburg PA
CBHW020312170426
43202CB00008B/578